THREE CASTLES BURNING

A HISTORY OF DUBLIN IN TWELVE STREETS

DONAL FALLON

NEW ISLAND

THREE CASTLES BURNING
First published in 2022 by
New Island Books
Glenshesk House
10 Richview Office Park
Clonskeagh
Dublin D14 V8C4
Republic of Ireland
www.newisland.ie

Print ISBN: 978-1-84840-872-2
eBook ISBN: 978-1-84840-873-9

British Library Cataloguing in Publication Data. A CIP catalogue record for this book is available upon request.

Set in 12 on 16 pt Bembo Std and
11.5 on 15.5 pt Adobe Garamond Pro

New Island Books is a member of Publishing Ireland

10 9 8 7 6 5 4 3 2

'This city,' says the tourist, 'presents the most extraordinary contrast of poverty and magnificence to be met in Europe.'

—William Curry, *Ancient and Modern Dublin* (1820)

To the memory of Joe Fallon

Many of the contemporary images in this book were taken on his vintage Nikon camera

Contents

Introduction

Why write a book about the streets of Dublin?

The dying months of 2021, and the opening months of the year which followed, were a curious time to be writing about the city Joyce christened the 'Hibernian Metropolis'. By then, there seemed to be a path emerging out of the global pandemic, which had brought all capital cities to a sudden and disorientating stop. That moment also reignited much discussion over what many of those cities could and should look like going forward. The greatest aspect of Dublin, Dermot Bolger argued in 1991, 'is not its buildings or history but the fact it is a living city. A city is like a person, it is always changing.'[1]

On the eve of the pandemic, there were some eighty new hotels in various stages of planning for the city. An unexpected consequence of the crisis internationally was the halting of other kinds of development, worsening a housing crisis of inadequate supply. When the cranes returned, Dubliners seemed to be asking, what would they be constructing?

Discussions on planning, the pre-eminence of hotels and student accommodation blocks and the place of cultural institutions in the capital have all taken hold in recent times. These discussions, and the renewed interest of Dubliners in their city and the form it takes, have sparked civic activism on a level not seen since Frank McDonald penned his important and vital book *The Destruction of Dublin* in 1985.

Three Castles Burning, a social history podcast founded in 2019, has aimed to be a voice which celebrates the heritage of the city, always within the context of the contemporary city. Many episodes, such as those exploring The O'Rahilly's Herbert Park home (demolished overnight in September 2020, leading the City Council to initiate legal action against the developer), have responded to on-going events in the city.

All cities must develop to grow, something that was believed by the pioneering figures of both Georgian and Victorian Dublin, as examined in this book. The balance of development is key. Cities ultimately require communities within them, and to be shaped by and for those who live there, while welcoming those who visit. The search for authenticity is what motivates much tourism.

I wished to write a book that would explore some of the streets of the capital, with potted histories that I hope will give visitors to the city a sense of its vast history, but which I primarily hope will give inspiration to those who call Dublin home. There are occasional heroic defeats here, like the Civic Offices' disputed construction at Wood Quay, but there are also moments of great civic achievement.

This is not intended as a guidebook, nor an architectural or academic history. Not one of these street histories could be considered truly definitive, stretching from the very beginning to the modern day and encompassing all that has happened there. Instead, I have presented the reader with a series of insights into each street that helps us understand its place in the contemporary city. Some streets are key in the history of ideas in the city, others to its development economically. Some of these streets are rapidly changing. Perhaps, like Flora Mitchell and her 1966 study *Vanishing Dublin,* which is referenced throughout this book, it seems an important time to capture them.

The centenary year of the publication of James Joyce's *Ulysses,* a masterpiece of literature that placed Dublin centre-stage, has been a reminder of Dublin's place internationally. The impact of this city on international thinking, culture and more besides is plentiful. She is no small town, and this is no small story.

In Dublin, like all great cities, the past and the present are in constant interaction with one another. It is also a time for thinking about the future.

Donal Fallon
Dublin 2022

1

Henrietta Street

Henrietta Street c.1970 (National Library of Ireland)

If one street can tell us of Dublin's rise and demise, it is Henrietta Street. It also has an unrivalled story of rebirth, a slice of Georgian Dublin reborn when so much was irreversibly lost. The most exclusive address in the Georgian city, it was initially home to what one authority on the street has described as, 'the leading figures from church, military and state, sophisticated socialites, agents of culture and arbiters of taste.'[1]

By the time of the 1911 Census, however, the street was a picture of poverty, with 835 people residing in just fifteen homes. In less than two centuries, subdivided tenements had replaced the fashionable abodes of the rich and powerful.

Henrietta Street, for a street so important in the development of the Irish capital, spends a lot of its time playing the role of somewhere else entirely. In the popular television series *Penny Dreadful*, a horror drama featuring characters like Dr Victor Frankenstein and a reimagined Dorian Gray, the cobbled street was used to evoke a feeling of place – but that place was Victorian London. Similarly, we see Henrietta Street in *Ripper Street*, a series which takes dramatic licence with the tale of London's most infamous killer, Jack the Ripper. Macabre walking tours take to the streets of Whitechapel and Spitalfields nightly in London, exploring the gruesome history and lore around the Ripper, but television production companies feel this Dublin street offers a better sense of Victorian London than that city itself can muster. To a resident of the street, it seems that, 'Henrietta Street has been used to represent the Dickensian squalor of London … It's not representing Dublin, it's not representing Ireland and it's a massive inconvenience to the local residents.'[2]

The prop red post boxes and the acting Victorian Bobbies come and go, but that Henrietta Street should be considered a quintessential London street is no doubt something its early residents would delight in. The emulation of the great city, the undisputed capital of the Empire, was a preoccupation of the Georgian Dubliner. To Jonathan Swift, who privately reckoned 'no man is thoroughly miserable unless he be condemned to live in Ireland', London represented a place of stimulating social and political life, and was worthy of not only admiring but copying:

> If you have London still at heart,
> We'll make a small one here by art;
> The difference is not much between
> St. James's Park, and Stephen's Green.[3]

Whatever the differences in her green spaces, Henrietta Street represented a direct imitation of the fashionable streets of the neighbouring metropolis by Dublin. With its two opposing rows of red-brick houses, and with a beautiful commonality on street level that conceals the unique decorated interiors behind each door, Henrietta

Street looked unlike anything the city had witnessed before. Dublin's first Georgian terraced street, it was to mark the beginning of a very real influence over the shaping of the eighteenth-century city by one Luke Gardiner.

A treasury official, parliamentarian and property developer – perhaps today someone we would label a property tycoon – the early life of Luke Gardiner remains something of a mystery, but his beginnings were seemingly relatively humble, being the son of a merchant. In a city where so many defined themselves by the pedigree of a family line or title, Gardiner was 'a self-made man of obscure origins'.[4] It was his marriage to Anne Stewart in 1711, niece to Viscount Mountjoy, a prominent Anglo-Irish peer, which opened doors in Georgian society, lending Gardiner what historian Melanie Hayes has described as 'a gloss of nobility'.[5]

While Gardiner's plan to develop Henrietta Street was ambitious, its development proved slow. Still, it was helped by the fact that the street's arrival in the 1720s coincided with the opening of a new parliament on College Green, which meant that the street attracted the political class from its infancy. Within three decades – by the time the final house on the street, number 3, was completed in the late 1750s – it was home to what David Dickson has termed 'a remarkable concentration of political power and factional rivalry within a small physical space.'[6] Gardiner did not live to see the street's completion, having died in 1755, but his sons would continue to play a central role in the development of Dublin's northside.

As for the origins of the street's name, it is somewhat disputed. Street names in the Georgian city often commanded a sense of power, with developers frequently bestowing their own names – or allusions to their titled positions – upon the streetscape. The most ludicrous example of this was the case of Earl Henry Moore of Drogheda, responsible for North Earl Street, Henry Street, Moore Street, Drogheda Street (which in time became Sackville Street and later O'Connell Street) and even Of Lane. Gardiner's new fashionable street was likely named in honour of Henrietta Paulet, Duchess of Bolton, wife (third wife, no less) of former Lord Lieutenant Charles Paulet, though some have suggested Henrietta Fitzroy, Duchess of Grafton. Either Henrietta would give the street a sense of exclusivity and a closeness to power, which was undoubtedly the desired effect.

Those who lived in these houses lived significant lives, yes, but what of those who laboured in them? Behind each wealthy household was a working staff. Mary Wollstonecraft, an early advocate of women's rights, whose 1792 text *A Vindication of the Rights of Woman* is considered one of the pioneering works of feminist philosophy, worked as governess to the daughters of the Kingsborough family in number 15 from 1786. Only 27 years of age at the time she assumed the post, Wollstonecraft had a life-long impact on Margaret, one of the children in her care, with historian Jenny McAuley writing that, 'Margaret energetically lived out Wollstonecraft's democratic and feminist ideals, becoming a major Irish Patriot hostess, and subsequently pursuing a literary career and the independent study of medicine.'[7]

★★★

Walking up Henrietta Street today from the busy Bolton Street, the houses have a commanding presence. An urban myth in many cities with such fine Georgian architecture has long maintained that the smaller windows of Georgian houses' upper floors were those of servants quarters, but in truth it tells us more about the architectural style of the Georgian period than any penny-pinching on the part of the wealthy. The smaller windows on the top floor gave the illusion of height, and contributed to the perceived scale of the homes.

But beyond the impressive homes themselves, the feeling of the street is also created by the cul-de-sac effect of having the King's Inns at its western end, along with the striking archway designed by Francis Johnston, an architect best remembered for the General Post Office and the doomed Nelson's Pillar. Dating from 1820, it is a powerful closing presence to the street, and above the archway we see the Royal Coat of

Arms, complete with a lion representing England and a unicorn for Scotland. This symbol of empire, ever-present in British cityscapes, is a rare thing in Dublin now, largely replaced upon independence. This cul-de-sac meant that unlike other inner-city streets, the people of Henrietta Street did not contend with the hustle and bustle of constant traffic. The street had its own unique soundscape.

The presence of King's Inns, a training institution for barristers of the law, would come to shape

Entrance to King's Inns, 1986 (Courtesy of Dublin City Library and Archive)

Henrietta Street itself, and provide it with something of a lifeline in a time of steep decline for the city. A street which drew the political class could hardly be expected to survive the shock of the Act of Union between Britain and Ireland in 1800, when the Irish Parliament voted for its own abolition. It was the end product of a parliament which, in the words of the eminent historian Lecky, fell victim to a 'virus of corruption which extended and descended through every fibre and artery of the political system'.[8]

The political effects of the Act of Union were obvious, with London assuming greater and more direct control over Irish affairs, but the economic effects of it in Dublin were more multifaceted. After the union, Thomas Pakenham noted, 'some people predicted that grass would grow in the streets of Dublin. The future was to be less theatrical.'[9] Many streets did quickly succumb to tenements, as parliamentarians and the economy that flourished around them and their social calendar left the city. More than 200 parliamentarians called Dublin home in 1800 – just six Irish MPs had Dublin addresses by 1823, less than a quarter of a century later.[10]

Henrietta Street found a new purpose for a time, directly connected to the presence of the King's Inns. Attorneys, barristers and judges were drawn to the street, which a nineteenth-century observer described as having 'the air of a legal university'.[11]

The great disruptor of this harmony – and perhaps the event which would most directly shape the future of the street – was the arrival of the Dublin Militia, a reserve force of the army intended to defend the capital, which took up residence in numbers 12 and 14 from 1863, in homes which essentially assumed the role of barracks. Soldiers, their families, and all the noise it entailed drove a wedge between the new arrivals and the legal profession, residents complaining of how concentration was impossible with the noise of soldiers drilling and the 'eternal drumming and fife by incipient musicians'.[12] The new busy-ness of Henrietta Street was controversial enough to make it to the British House of Commons, where parliamentarians heard of how Henrietta Street, 'was made a perpetual play-ground not only by the children of the Militia but by numbers attracted from the district to participate with the Militia children in their uncontrolled games and sports, to the great obstruction of the street.'[13]

The sound of children playing on the street survived the eventual departure of the Militia for barracks accommodation elsewhere in the city. For a street so synonymous with tenement Dublin, Henrietta Street did not house a single tenement before the transformation of number 14, from a home of soldiers to a subdivided warren of homes within a home towards the end of the nineteenth century. Businessman Thomas Vance acquired number 14 in 1877, the first tenement of the street and today home to a museum that tells the story of the street through its various ages. Vance's home was a tenement, but it was far removed from the worst such home until the 1870s. Toilets were to be found on multiple landings, a vast improvement on the yard toilets still common then in inner-city Dublin. There was to be 'an oven for each family, and the provision of clean running water, again provided on each landing'.[14]

Tenements, at their heart, were subdivided homes designed to provide cheap rental accommodation. There was nothing uniquely Dublin about the presence of such homes in the city, tenements being a fact of life in all major cities in these islands. In Edinburgh and Glasgow, tenements were generally purpose-built structures that reflected industrial might and the need for workers in cities. They were, and still are, desirable properties. A journalist in *The Times* wrote in recent times of how 'there is no denying Scotland's love affair with tenements'.[15]

Yet the scale of tenement Dublin was something that could not be ignored, reflecting the broader decay of the nineteenth-century city. There was also a sad uniqueness in their origin story. These were not purpose-built working-class homes, as described above, but something else entirely. To *The Irish Builder*, an authoritative voice on matters of planning and construction:

> The history and fate of thousands of fine old well-built private mansions in Dublin is a chequered and

sad one – for go where you will, either north and south of this city, streets of houses will be found now occupied as tenements. The evil is yearly enlarging and there are large districts now possible of being mapped out where this tenement property has become long blocks and lines of rookeries and chronic fever-nests. The evil has grown so gigantic that the Corporation [Dublin Corporation, the local authority] are powerless to grapple with it in its entirety.[16]

Vance's efforts on the street were little by comparison to Alderman Joseph M. Meade, a councillor who would later serve as Lord Mayor of the city twice. Meade acquired the majority of houses on the street, which by this point no longer held strong appeal to legal professionals, subdividing them and renting them out. A self-described Irish nationalist and a supporter of Irish Parliamentary Party leader Charles Stewart Parnell, Meade was by no means unique in local municipal politics as a tenement landlord, but the scale of his holdings on Henrietta Street sets him apart from most of his contemporaries.

We can gather some idea of life on Henrietta Street from the census returns of the early twentieth century, which reveal the layers of working-class life on the street. Taking just one home from the 1911 census, 7 Henrietta Street, we find 104 people within the home, with occupations as varied as tailor, domestic servant, porter,

Mural of James Joyce on Henrietta Street (Luke Fallon)

carpenter, a post office worker, and general labourer. The sheer number of children is striking, and recalls the words of James Joyce in the pages of *Dubliners*, where we read of Little Chandler, a character who embarks across the city from an office at the King's Inns and makes for the city centre via this street, which is packed with children:

> He emerged from under the feudal arch of the King's Inns, a neat modest figure, and walked swiftly down Henrietta Street. The golden sunset was waning and the air had grown sharp. A horde of grimy children populated the street. They stood or ran in the roadway or crawled up the steps before

the gaping doors or squatted like mice upon the thresholds. Little Chandler gave them no thought. He picked his way deftly through all that minute vermin-like life and under the shadow of the gaunt spectral mansions in which the old nobility of Dublin had roystered.[17]

Depiction of a Dublin tenement stairwell, and landlord, from *The Lepracaun Cartoon Monthly* (Courtesy of Dublin City Library and Archive)

In revolutionary times, from 1916–21, Henrietta Street and other streets like it contributed their share of young radicals. Patrick Farrell, an apprentice plasterer and just nineteen years of age, would lose his life in the fierce fighting at nearby Church Street during the 1916 Rising. He was raised in 14 Henrietta Street, although lived in Parnell Street at the time of the Rising. There were others from the street killed during the Easter Week rebellion, the *Sinn Féin Rebellion Handbook* recording a 58-year-old 'D. Dargan' of 12 Henrietta Street as amongst the civilians buried in Glasnevin that week, along with young James Gibney, just 5 years of age, from neighbouring Henrietta Place. Amongst the deported prisoners after the failure of the uprising was a 'J. Monahan' of 5 Henrietta Street, and a 'J. Summers' of number 7.

The street witnessed the very real excitement of a significant IRA arms raid in the summer of 1920 during the Irish War of Independence, at a time when the republican movement was seeking desperately to arm itself in the city by any means necessary. The King's Inns armoury, guarded by a small band of British soldiers and intended to protect an institution of the law, was identified by the leadership of the IRA as being not only likely to reap dividends, but also to be potentially lightly protected. For Denis Holmes, a young IRA Volunteer who participated in the subsequent raid, the abiding memory of the raid was Kevin Barry 'coming out of the guardroom with a Lewis gun hugged in his arms'.[18] Barry, within a few short months, was an international cause célèbre, executed at eighteen years of age in Mountjoy Prison for his role in an ambush at an intersection of Church Street and North King Street that led to the deaths of three British soldiers.

Holmes recalled that the IRA had watched the King's Inns for some time, as: 'our GHQ [General Headquarters] had learnt through the intelligence department that although the Inns were well guarded, military discipline was not so strict as it was in other outposts.' The daring raid on King's Inns involved other men mobilising in the vicinity of Henrietta Street, with Holmes recounting that, 'a party in Henrietta Street … was standing ready to protect the men on the raid.' Volunteers 'formed a cordon across Henrietta Street, and did not leave their position until all our men had got safely away'.[19]

Later, there was the execution of Thomas Bryan, a 24-year-old electrician from number 14 who was a member of the IRA's Active Service Unit in the capital. While the War of Independence was raging in the countryside, the ASU fought a very different war on the streets of the capital. Bryan was part of a botched ambush at Drumcondra in January 1921, for which he was hanged at Mountjoy Prison. A young, recently married man, correspondence in his pension application submitted by his grieving family reveals the poverty in which his parents continued to live at 14 Henrietta Street in the aftermath of his death.

This being the heart of working-class Dublin, there were also local men who enlisted in the First World War effort. Indeed, it reflects the economic reality of Henrietta Street that it contributed more men to the British armed forces than to the ranks of the IRA. Conor Dodd, a historian with special interest in the Royal Dublin Fusiliers, has detailed the contribution of the street to the regiment. There was Corporal Thomas Gormley of number 13, who received a Distinguished Conduct Medal for gallantry, leading a group of twenty men in an attack on an enemy machine gun position. From number 14, the same home as the Bryan family, came Patrick Ennis. A father to two children, Patrick worked as a general labourer, like so many underemployed men in a city of little industrial prospect. He enlisted in the summer of 1914. He was present at Gallipoli, and later at the Western Front, where 1916 came to mean something very different to those at home. Patrick survived the war, making it back to 14 Henrietta Street. However, not all of the residents of this street who went to war made it home.[20]

***

The Henrietta Street that emerged after the birth of the Irish Free State was, at first, little changed from before. The street, readers of the *Irish Independent* were told, 'was once the most fashionable and exclusive street in Dublin. Dukes and Lords paraded and great ladies graced the pavements where the barefooted, ragged urchins today are romping.'[21]

Post-independence, many wondered what real change would be brought about for the inner-city of the capital. A new wave of agitation on housing had taken hold from the time of a 1914 inquiry into Dublin housing, and now there existed a new state to make good on promises of improved conditions, and those words were still ringing in the ears of the city.

John Cooke, Honorary Treasurer of the National Society for the Prevention of Cruelty to Children (NSPCC), photographed Dublin's tenement landscape, including Henrietta Street and the neighbouring Henrietta Place, in the early years of the twentieth century with an eye not only for urban decay but the social realities of poverty. Cooke's photography was driven by a desire to put this poverty centre-stage, telling the aforementioned 1914 inquiry that:

> I condemn the whole of the tenement system now existing. It breeds misery; and worse. It causes a great waste of human life and human force; men, women and children can never rise to the best that is in them under such conditions.[22]

Some progress, in terms of brick and mortar, did gradually come. In place of that poverty which so shocked Cooke in Henrietta Place, for example, now stands Henrietta House, a public housing scheme dating from 1937 with the distinctive Art Deco flourishes that mark the work of Herbert George Simms, Housing Architect to Dublin Corporation from 1932 until 1948. Henrietta House has the fine rounded corners that mark out so many of Herbert Simms' schemes across the city, and consists of two blocks of flats facing a communal courtyard. Gone were crowded tenements and makeshift homes, replaced by the clean elegance of Henrietta House.

Around the corner, however, tenement living continued on Henrietta Street itself. The old houses of north inner-city Dublin, to one 1940s visitor, made a contradictory spectacle:

> Magnificent panelled doors, patched and burst and drunkenly hanging awry; delicately proportioned

Henrietta House in 1980, photographed from Henrietta Street
(Courtesy of Dublin City Library and Archive)

fanlights now devoid of glass; smashed and never-repaired panes and sashes in the windows; scaling paintwork; empty gaps and heaps of rubble that represent not the fall of a land-mine, but some half-hearted attempt at slum clearance.[23]

Two decades on, a visitor to Henrietta Street itself in the mid-1960s felt moved to write:

A small boy, when asked if he was afraid of anything going up the now ricketty staircases in the dark, replied instantly 'I'm in dread of ghosts!' One can only suppose that his feelings would be nothing in comparison with the horror of any returning ghosts.[24]

By the 1970s, the door of the last tenement home closed, and the future of the street – in spite of its past – seemed bleak. Newspapers spoke of the street as being amongst the 'last decaying bastions of Dublin's north city Georgian heritage'.[25]

By then, there was an increasing realisation that such houses should be saved, and could embark on new lives. An unlikely champion of the street, and Dublin's Georgian heritage more broadly, was Uinseann MacEoin, a republican and former veteran of the Curragh internee camp of the Second World War, which the De Valera government had utilised to contain the IRA and its network during the conflict. Some had scoffed at, and openly championed, the demolition of Dublin's Georgian heritage on the basis it was alien to the built landscape, little more than a relic of colonialism and British taste. When two impressive Georgian houses on Kildare Place were destroyed in August 1957, situated beside the National Museum of Ireland and within feet of the Dáil, one government minister insisted that, 'I was glad to see them go. They stood for everything I hate.'[26]

MacEoin felt otherwise. He was more than just a republican; he served as editor of the influential *Build* and *Plan* magazines, platforms for important voices in the emerging debates on planning and the city in the 1960s. Together with his wife Margaret, Uinseann began acquiring properties in the heart of the old Gardiner estate that many felt were only fit for demolition. On Henrietta Street, they first acquired number 5, a building which was home to seventy-five people when Uinseann first visited it in 1966, 'twelve of whom were living in the former drawing room, while the whole house shared one toilet. The landlord no longer wanted the property as he could not afford its upkeep due to rent restrictions.'[27]

MacEoin proceeded to turn the rooms of the house – which he acquired for a token sum – into artists' studios, a process he would replicate with other homes on the street. This coincided with the movement of many of the final tenants to new suburbia, and demonstrated that the story of the street did not have to end with their departure.

MacEoin's presence can still be seen on the street – 5 Henrietta Street is named James Bryson House, a plaque still bearing that name on its front wall. One would be forgiven for presuming Bryson to be a Georgian aristocrat for whom this was home. In truth, James Bryson was a high profile IRA Volunteer, who escaped from custody at the Crumlin Road courthouse in Belfast in February 1973, aged 24. He was shot dead in August. Less than a year later, MacEoin had renamed this Henrietta Street house in his honour. It was an unusual political gesture amongst Dublin's Georgian preservationists. Another plaque tells the story of the house, though it has almost entirely faded with the passing of time. It detailed the Georgian developers and owners of the home, but concludes 'Is Saoranach Éireann anois é'. These words are now all that remain visible. Translated, the plaque is proclaiming the house itself to be a citizen of Ireland. As historian Erika Hanna rightly notes, it was: 'a self-conscious integration of Ireland's two traditions and a symbolic baptism of the house into the nation's history.'[28]

The commitment of the MacEoin family to the street served as something of a catalyst in its renewal. To the former tenement homes of the street came some of the finest artists of the 1970s and subsequent decades, including Brian Maguire, Eithne Jordan, Cathy Carman and Charles Cullen. It was Cullen who introduced Mick O'Dea, formerly president of the Royal Hibernian Academy, to MacEoin and the studio spaces of the street. O'Dea recounted:

Our landlord, Uinseann MacEoin, was a town-planner, architect, conservationist, Republican, communist, family man, and admirer of the Anglo-Irish contribution, as well as being a writer, historian and mountain climber. He was an extraordinary man. He felt it was his duty as a citizen to let out studios cheaply to artists. It is he who is responsible for Henrietta Street becoming the home and hub of so many artists that it is today.[29]

MacEoin's belief in the street and its potential was shared by others too, like the artist Alice Hanratty and trade unionist Sé Geraghty, whose remarkable collection of books, described as an 'extensive library that encompassed the arts, literature, politics and history, with particular emphasis on old Dublin', was generously donated to the people of Dublin after his passing.[30] On the other side of the street, the Casey family turned number 13 into a family home which remained faithful to the past, acquired in 1974 with the help of an interest-free loan from the Irish Georgian Society. To Michael Casey, speaking on RTÉ's *Arts Express*, 'the idea is to restore the house, and to restore it as accurately as it can be restored.'[31]

Architectural restoration and preservation are not the only respected traditions on the street, with Na Píobairí Uilleann – committed to the preservation of Ireland's historic piping tradition – calling number 15 home. Established in 1968, the founding constitution of the body noted that, 'the main object of Na Píobairí Uilleann shall be the promotion generally of Irish music and the music of the uilleann pipes in particular.' It is sometimes possible to hear the sound of those pipes on the streets today, a historic instrument that recalls talents like Séamus Ennis, Breandán Breathnach and Leo Rowsome. This melting pot of people – pipers, painters, preservationists – all found what they needed in the Henrietta Street of the 1970s, when others felt the street had little future.

★★★

Just as Henrietta Street was beginning this new chapter in its existence, television cameras arrived in 1980, transforming the street into Chandler's Court, the fictional setting of James Plunkett's *Strumpet City*. A literary snapshot of bubbling class tensions, Plunkett's masterpiece was a tale of poverty, resilience and heroism set against the backdrop of the 1913 Lockout, a protracted labour dispute in the city which pitted the Dublin Employers Federation against the trade unionist Jim Larkin. In Plunkett's own words, he set out to depict a time when Dublin's working class, 'occupied the cast-off houses of the rich and they walked about – for the most part – in the cast-off clothes of the middle class.'[32] A street that has so often played the part of London was brilliantly utilised to bring that story to life, just a decade after the last residents had left the tenement homes. In trying to capture its appeal, Garrett Fagan has written:

> Tenements were still a significant feature of the city when the TV series aired in 1980. However the success of the book is perhaps partly due to its recording of a way of life that was passing away. In a movement from margins to centre, as the reality of the Tenements faded from view, their place in the city's imagination and sense of itself grew.[33]

The place of these houses in the imagination of the city is certainly real. The 14 Henrietta Street Museum, which tells the story of the street from its Georgian beginnings to its tenement subdivision, is colloquially known in the city as the 'Tenement Museum', despite its intentions of telling a much broader narrative.[34] Tenements occupied this street from the time of Thomas Vance acquiring that very building in the 1870s until the final residents departed it in the 1970s. While there was much history before, and much revival since, that century is what has come to define Henrietta Street in the eyes of the city.

2

Watling Street

In the Liberties, a so-called 'Guinness Man' was most desirable to any bachelorette, for he came not only with a healthy pension but some of the finest labour privileges in the city. So it was for my grandmother, the daughter of a British Army soldier from Cornmarket, who wed a young Guinness employee in the 1950s. Fionn Davenport, author of a colourful and entertaining guide book to the city, tells his readers that 'in the nineteenth century, young women of marrying age in Dublin were advised by their mothers to get their hands on a Guinness Man.' The policy remained the same into subsequent decades.[1]

In a city of deeply precarious and unpredictable work, Guinness offered the rarest of things to Dublin's working class: stability. There was a paternalism that extended from the cradle to the grave, and even beyond it, with widows' pensions and more besides. Brewery workers, trade union historian Francis Devine has wryly noted, were not to be found 'in the vanguard of labour'.[2] Many workers in Dublin had cause for righteous anger, but there was little of it within the walls of the brewery. As one local recalled it, the existing local order was kind to them:

> In the social hierarchy of the Liberties the publicans were at the top. Next to them shopkeepers jostled for position, and third were the tradesmen, bakers, carpenters, bricklayers and others. Lowest of all were the labourers, with one exception: the labourers who worked in Guinness. They were in a class of their own, never knew broken employment, and worked with the conscious air of belonging to the world's largest brewery.[3]

My grandfather was – the Guinness genealogy archive tells me – a 'tank process man', which sounds considerably less romantic than a Guinness Man. Nonetheless, it made him a small yet important cog in the enormous machine that was a brewery without equal in these islands. He was just 24 on entering the brewery in 1948, fresh-faced from a stint pouring pints in the public houses of London as the Blitz happened outside the pub door and overhead.

The job of such workers, in the ever-expanding Container Department of the company, centred on moving Guinness from the brewery itself to the 'Plain People of Ireland'. Until the 1950s, they filled wooden casks with

stout. By the 1960s, they were filling enormous transport-
able tanks, each containing some 3,000 pints. They were
cleaned out, filled up, and sent on their way.

Standing at the intersection of Watling Street and
James's Street, the extent of the contemporary Guinness
brewery – and other Diageo outposts – is clear. The
famed entrance gate to the brewery is visible, an archway on which the establishment year of the company is
displayed on one side, and the contemporary year on the
other. Each year, a modest crowd gathers by the corner
of Watling Street to cheer Guinness employee Robbie
Minto as one year is replaced with another. 'I remember
when the guy used to stand on the other fella's shoulders
while he was painting that,' an observer commented in
recent years, 'now you have to have a machine to get up
there.'[4] Alas, gone is the painter too, but the more modern
plaques still fulfil the same purpose, telling us something:
we as a city, and Guinness as an enterprise, are still here.

No company has so successfully advertised its way into
our collective psyche as Guinness. Not only is the name of
the founder of the company instantly recognisable, but so is
its foundation year, 1759. The product, however, is significantly younger. In its infancy, the brewery Arthur Guinness
established produced ale, then the dominant drink in the city.
Eighteenth-century wits thought little of Dublin's offering:

The beer is sour – thin, musty, thick and stale
And worse than anything except the ale.[5]

The success of Guinness was not merely that it came to produce a superior product, in the form of porter, but that its founding father almost immediately set his sights on the world beyond these shores. As the definitive economic history of the company notes, 'Guinness's brewery can no more be considered solely in an Irish context than can the Irish economy be considered as an autonomous unit. Guinness grew to straddle the Irish Sea.'[6]

But whatever of global dominance, what about the immediate neighbourhood? The Liberties district came to dominate several of Dublin's most important industries, including brewing and distilling. By the middle of the eighteenth century, the city was capable of sustaining some forty breweries, many small in scale, while almost thirty distilleries had emerged by the 1780s.[7] We can wonder how only one of these eighteenth-century enterprises remains in business at the same location. Many will point to the strength of the product, but a building near the corner of Watling Street reveals something else.

★★★

The Rupert Guinness Theatre, opened in May 1951, was designed by Guinness architect R. J. Bickford, to the plans of W. D. Robertson, the chief engineer of the brewery. Though a modern building out of kilter with much of the Georgian fabric of neighbouring James's

The Rupert Guinness Theatre (Luke Fallon)

Street, it is also a fitting reminder of the cultural and societal impact of the Guinness brewery on the Liberties. Guinness' philanthropy led to the construction of homes, indoor markets and public parks within walking distance of the brewery, but culture had its place too.

Within weeks of the theatre opening, the Abbey Theatre on the other side of the Liffey endured a fire which put its primary stage beyond use – and the worlds of Yeast and Yeats met, as the national theatre temporarily relocated itself to the centre of Guinness Dublin. On seeing the new Guinness theatre after the blaze, the Abbey's Artistic Director Ria Mooney was moved to say, 'it is like coming out of a bad dream.'[8]

With the ability to seat 600 people, and level oak floors which allowed it to be utilised as a dancehall, the theatre thrived as the centre of cultural life in the company, providing a home to the Guinness Choir and the Guinness Players. Productions by the latter included Samuel Beckett's *Waiting For Godot,* something which would have appealed to Beckett himself no doubt – 'I'm a dab hand at pouring Guinness,' he recounted on one occasion to a struggling host.[9] The Guinness Players brought some truly unique productions to Dublin audiences, like John Osborne's kitchen-sink realist drama *Look Back in Anger,* and Henrik Ibsen's *A Doll House.* For a period, there was more diversity in the offerings of the Guinness Players than those of the national theatre who had temporarily taken up residence in their home.

★★★

Another piece of twentieth-century architecture which commands attention on Watling Street are the Emmet Buildings flats, designed by City Housing Architect Herbert George Simms and his team, which opened in November 1937.

Simms, a working-class Londoner and a veteran of the Royal Field Artillery and the First World War, had studied architecture at Liverpool University in the aftermath of the conflict, a door that was opened to him by an ex-service scholarship of tuition fees and princely sum of £150 for three years. By 1932, he was appointed the first dedicated Housing Architect of Dublin Corporation, a significant departure for a city where housing – and just about everything else – had fallen under the brief of the City Architect. The establishment of a specific office to tackle the housing crisis head-on was an acknowledgement of the scale of the problem.

Like so many of his works across the city, the Watling Street flats have Art Deco flourishes, visible in their curves, gates and other architectural features. Many see Amsterdam and Rotterdam in this scheme, and other instantly recognisable Simms designs across the city, but he was equally influenced by trends in working-class housing in Britain. The time in which Simms worked recalls massive suburban expansion like Cabra and Crumlin, but the Watling Street flats and others like them reflected a belief that people could and should live in the city too. Blocks of four-storey flats facing shared inner-courtyards, communal stairwells and balconies overseeing shared spaces are all features of Simms' developments in the city.

The first residents to move into the Watling Street flats were families from nearby Marrowbone Lane, another street which would witness his architectural impact in time, and to which some of them returned. This was reflective of the favoured policy of 'decanting', whereby, 'tenants were temporarily evacuated from slum tenements, the tenements demolished, blocks of new flats built, and the evacuated tenements rehoused in the new flats.'[10] Others remained in Emmet Buildings, where a strong sense of community developed. These flats were not merely an architectural success, but a victory for the very idea that inner-city living was not only possible but desirable. Watling Street, blighted by tenements in earlier decades, now housed the modernist vision of Simms.

Simms brought real honesty to discussions on housing in the city. Speaking before a Housing Inquiry in City Hall in 1939, he was adamant that, 'housing of the working classes would have to be accepted sooner or later as a permanent service, like water or other municipal services'. When questioned on the lifespan of flats by the same inquiry, he insisted that flats 'if properly maintained and not abused should last 200 years, which was longer than the life of the slum dwellings they were replacing.'[11]

Simms is an increasingly admired figure in the contemporary city, perhaps reflecting modern frustrations around housing. If we could do it then, some ask, why not now? It is undoubtedly difficult not to be moved by the story of his commitment to housing the poor of the city, but also by the tragic nature of his death by suicide in 1948, which came after a period in which he was undoubtedly overworked. The retirement of Dublin's City Architect, Horace O'Rourke, in 1945 had left Simms balancing the workloads of two men and two offices. At breaking point, he left a note that captured his own frustrations at the scale of the work before him:

I cannot stand it any longer, my brain is too tired
to work any more. It has not had a rest for 20 years
except when I am in heavy sleep. It is always on the
go like a dynamo and still the work is being piled
on to me.[12]

Newfound admiration for Simms in our time is also a
reflection of the increasing awareness of the twentieth-
century-built landscape, and the recognised place of
modernist designs like his schemes. We no longer see
the city as a Georgian jewel with pockets of Victorian
elegance, but as something much more diverse. Still, as
geographer and Simms authority Ruth McManus has
rightly acknowledged, the beauty of these schemes on
street level does not mean they are without fault. There
was an acknowledgement, even in the 1930s, that the
dwellings were small. Simms himself, McManus believes,
'would have been quick to acknowledge the need to
provide residents with updated facilities. Retrofitting
to modern standards, although expensive, can provide
for these needs while appropriately respecting our
architectural heritage. It is also, as is increasingly recognised, more environmentally sound than new builds.'[13]

The naming of the Simms blocks across the city
reflected the nationalist politics of the Corporation.
Markievicz House and Pearse House honoured heroes of
more recent history, but in the Liberties – an area which
had been at the centre of planning the 1798 insurrection

and the United Irish conspiracy more broadly – Emmet Buildings would be joined by the nearby Oliver Bond scheme, named in honour of, like Robert Emmet, a member of the United Irish leadership. More important than the historic legacies they honoured, however, was their contemporary impact and, when development plans for Watling Street were first announced, one newspaper went as far as to say that, 'with the passing of this slum another eyesore will be removed from the city, and another triumph achieved through the progressive policy of the Corporation.'[14] Reading the word 'slum' utilised in describing the street may seem surprising, but it is in line with the recollections of Liberties writer Lar Redmond, looking back on the 1920s and 1930s:

> A lot of nostalgic nonsense has been written in recent years about the Liberties, but the Liberties of my boyhood was a place of stark want where the evil spirit of the Gorta [a reference to the Famine, translating as 'the Hunger'] stalked every street.[15]

Of course, Simms' Art Deco designs were not the only eye-catching structures on the street. In view too, alongside the Emmet Buildings, is the imposing windmill of what was once Dublin's most successful distillery.

The Roe distillery had its origins in the 1750s, making it an exact contemporary of Guinness. Initially a humble distillery founded by Peter Roe, under the stewardship of George Roe from the 1830s – and renamed George Roe & Co – it grew to occupy a site of some seventeen acres.

We get some idea of the lavishness of the Roe distillery from the first-hand account of Alfred Barnard, Victorian

The Harp magazine image of St Patrick's Windmill (Thanks to Guinness Archive)

historian of brewing and distilling who embarked on a thirsty research trip that brought him through four English distilleries, twenty-eight Irish ones and a remarkable 129 Scottish distilleries, all in the name of *The Whisky Distilleries of the United Kingdom*, a snapshot of an industry in the mid-1880s. Barnard's book, now recognised as the definitive eye-witness account of Victorian distilling, is full of interesting colour on Dublin, for example describing the first sights that greeted his party in stepping off their boat from Scotland:

> On arrival at the North Wall we disembarked, when we beheld a sight which caused us much merriment. Jaunting cars rattled up to the wharf one after the other, their drivers arrayed in an assortment of garments from every old clothes shop in the Kingdom … We secured one of the best of the shabby looking cars, and although the horse was somewhat gone in the legs, he rattled us along so fast that some of us had to hold on to the straps, to prevent being pitched into the dusty street … Before we left the 'Charmin' City' we got quite attached to these rollicking drivers, and preferred outside cars to any other mode of conveyance.[16]

Of course, what Barnard describes here is poverty, in a city of little industrial strength, not least when compared to the

Clydeside he had just left. There was one Irish industrial powerhouse that could contend with Scotland however, and that is what concerned him. Barnard found in Roe's a distillery capable of producing some two million gallons of spirits a year, and noted how 'the entrance to the establishment is most striking and unlike any other distilleries we have seen, reminding us of some of the chateaux in France, with their ivy-covered walls and flower beds.'[17]

Even by the time of Barnard's visit, the striking windmill of the distillery was a historic curiosity, no longer in use. Visible from Watling Street as well as Thomas Street, the smock windmill (once the largest of its kind in Europe) could power a distillery in the eighteenth century, but lost purpose, though never presence, over time. Complete with a copper-domed roof and weather vane of St Patrick, patron saint of Ireland, it is a cherished reminder of the industrial heritage of what was once the epicentre of Irish distilling. While the sails of the windmill were removed at the time that steam replaced wind as the primary means of power, Patrick has withstood all change.

Is it Patrick at all? In the pages of *The Harp*, the in-house magazine of the Guinness brewery, it was noted that:

We are accepting this as a figure of Ireland's patron saint, and not of St. James (whom some loyal St. James's Gate people affirm it to be) in the admitted absence of any final evidence of identity, but in the firm believe [*sic.*] that our forebears are more likely

to have chosen Patrick to give a silent blessing to our
land at all points of the compass, in the traditional
Patrician attitude of this figure.[18]

The magazine showed coppersmith Patrick Dorrington
and apprentice Tony Cousins affixing Patrick in place. At
the time *The Harp* printed this image in 1958, the public
houses of the city still closed on St Patrick's Day.

★★★

At Watling Street's intersection with Bonham Street, and
taking up plenty of both streets, is an enormous bonded
store, typical of a nineteenth-century warehouse. Its
large loading doors are still visible, though covered up.
This building is one surviving part of the Roe Empire
and distillery that closed its doors in 1923.

If the empty bonded stores of Roe's on one side of the
street tell the story of the decline of a company – one which
buckled under the pressure of Temperance, prohibition (in
far-off places) and tariffs – the other side of Watling Street
is dominated by the success of Guinness. The brewery has
grown towards the Liffey, swallowing up what was once the
site of its leading rival, the Phoenix Brewery. Established
in 1778 by London brewer Samuel Madder, Phoenix produced a porter which was of a high and praised standard.
All that doomed the company was Madder's own failures
as a businessman, amassing enormous debts. The brewery
was later acquired by Daniel O'Connell Junior, son of the

famed parliamentary leader, who proved every bit as inef-
fective as Madder in running a brewery. None of the new
proprietors, economic historians have noted, 'knew anything of business or indeed of brewing, and their porter,
despite the Liberator's high testimony to its quality, was
usually unsaleable.'[19] O'Connell Ale was sometimes cyni-
cally presented as a Catholic alternative to the 'Protestant
Porter' of Arthur Guinness & Sons, but a superior product
and a rich legacy of philanthropy ensured the continued
loyalty of a city to the better product.

The Phoenix Brewery suffered from financial mis-
management, but what of other opponents? David
Dickson attributes the rise of the Guinness Company, in
part, to its ruthless competitiveness, noting that 'the brewery broke out of its original four-acre site in the 1850s
and expanded ten-fold in the next two decades, colonis-
ing a vast brown-field site between James Street and the
Liffey.'[20] Offering things like free delivery within a ten-
mile radius and 'keeping an army of dray-horses busy',
Guinness dominance was hard won. There was a sense
of inevitability in the fall of each opponent, even as they
looked to find a commercial angle off their competition
with the behemoth that was Guinness – The Phoenix
Brewery slogan boasted that it was *The Largest Brewery
in Ireland (but One)*. When the Phoenix Brewery disappeared, the nearby D'Arcy's brewery proclaimed itself to
be *The Largest Brewery in Ireland (but One)*. When D'Arcy's
folded, no surviving brewery adopted the ominous boast.

Surviving contemporary commentary on the fall of the other Dublin breweries paints a picture of the successful brewery as a sort of fantastical character, swallowing up all around it. Periodical *The Lepracaun,* which satirised Dublin society and politics in the early twentieth century, was an equal opportunities offender. None escaped its ire, from trade union leaders to city Aldermen, and from suffragettes to captains of industry like Guinness. In one instance, cartoonist Thomas Fitzpatrick captured the impossible task of competing with Guinness, even including the sad sight of other breweries – perhaps those of Watling Street – listed as 'to let'.

On the same side of the street as the brewery, and near the Bonham Street intersection, is the curious ghost sign of the Central Hide and Skin Company, a tannery which occupied numbers 49–53 into the living memory of the city. Today, the abiding smells of Watling Street and its surrounding area are the production of Guinness: roasted barley and hops both have their own distinctive smells, known to those who live in not only the Liberties but surrounding areas like Rialto, and across the river in Stoneybatter. However, for a considerable period of time in the history of the street, the smell of skinners and tanners, like the Central Hide and Skin Company, was considerably less welcome but equally familiar, at least in the immediate area. A glance at *Thom's Directory* for 1862 reveals a street of such companies, with ten listed tanners on the street, not to mention glue makers and leather curriers.

The Lepracaun comments on Guinness dominance (Courtesy of Dublin City library & Archive)

In an area in which animals were so important to the commercial success of enterprises like breweries and distilleries, animals played a less romantic role in the economic history of this street. The presence of such industries owed much to the Liffey being so well supplied with water, with the proximity of the River Poddle to the east and the Camac to the west. As a result, it has been noted that, 'the industries which grew up during the eighteenth century tended to be those which could take advantage of this useful raw material.'[21]

Watling Street is something of a microcosm of the economic story of the Liberties, what with the remnants of tanneries and the evidence of former distilleries in the view of Roe's windmill and the surviving bonded stores. A stroll through the Liberties reveals that the later industry is thankfully returning, as part of what some have termed a renaissance of Irish whiskey. Within a short walking distance of Watling Street are Pearse Lyons, Teeling, the Dublin Liberties Distillery and Roe & Co, the last a resurrection of the historic name of George Roe's business. There is a degree of irony in that new arrival being a product of Diageo. A former rival of Guinness, socially at least, now part of the broader portfolio ambitions of its parent company.

★★★

The ghost signage of the Central Hide and Skin Company
(Luke Fallon)

One group of people who are familiar with the name of Watling Street are swimmers, the Guinness wharf beside the bridge linking the street to Ellis Street on the northside marking the traditional beginning point of the Liffey Swim. The Guinness barges may be gone from the river, but the race has remained (mostly) faithful to its starting point.[22]

Twenty-seven men began the first Liffey Swim on 22 July 1920, the competitive event owing its existence to Dublin Corporation engineer Bernard Fagan, who himself finished third. Even in those earliest days, as revolution played out in the city, the swim attracted an audience of curious onlookers. Alfred Burgess, brother of the revolutionary leader Cathal Brugha, recalled watching the swim during the War of Independence, and looking across the river to spot his brother over the windows of a shop on the quays: 'Under Lalor's was a lorry load of Auxiliaries, and in one of the windows in Lalor's was Cathal, looking out of the window at the Liffey Swim also.'[23] The hunters and the hunted, all finding time to watch the spectacle.

The Liffey Swim recalls the painting of Jack B. Yeats by the same name, depicting large crowds gazing over the Liffeyside walls. The iconic work claimed a silver medal at the Summer Olympic Games of 1924. Technically brilliant,

1970s image of Rory O'More Bridge at the bottom of Watling Street. The starting point of the Liffey Swim. (Courtesy of Dublin City Library and Archive)

the work, 'showed the strong, confident, transitional style, no outlines, broad, long brush strokes, rich colour: the whole painted with great rapidity.'[24] It has commanded the imagination of many participants in the race, 2015 winner Donncha Ó Siadhail recalling how he encountered a copy of it in the hospital where his child was born: 'On the third floor, as I was walking down to meet him, there's a picture of the Liffey Swim just up on the wall. Every year I'm in the Liffey, I'm thinking of that painting.'[25] Terence de Vere White, friend of the painter, would ponder how strange it felt, 'with so little genius to go around, that Dublin should have withheld so long from according to Yeats the painter what it had granted to Yeats the poet.'[26] The painter, and more specifically *The Liffey Swim* as a piece of work, is now ingrained in the mind of the city.

The excitement that Yeats captures in that painting is reflected in the newspaper reports of the decade in which he painted it. In his painting we see a packed tram looking down on proceedings, not unlike this 1920s observation:

> From windows and roads the progress of the competitors was keenly watched, and hundreds of people availed of lorries, motor cars, hackney cars, in fact, vehicles of every description, to view the swimmers. Youngsters evinced no trepidation in taking up hazardous positions on the ladders leading to the river and on the parapets of bridges. Their enthusiasm

was unbounded, and with them the Liffey Swim is an event that is eagerly anticipated each year.[27]

There is not only great excitement around Watling Street and Victoria Quay each year of the swim, there is also the sense of continuity, and even commemoration. Many partake in the event because their own loved ones had done it before them. In the 1950s, Jack Fagan claimed victory, an honour befitting the son of the race founder.

Unsurprisingly, given the proximity of the race to the brewery, and the emphasis on physical fitness and sporting recreation with the company, Guinness employees have a long history of participation in the race. Its youngest winner, 1966's Francis 'Chalkie' White, was just 11 years old. The son of a Guinness employee, he represented the Guinness Swimming Club.

Whatever about 11-year-old boys, the idea of women jumping into the water by Watling Street was too much for some. In the pages of the *Irish Press* in February 1943, Dublin's Catholic Archbishop, the omnipotent John Charles McQuaid, maintained that with regards athletics and sports, 'mixed athletics and all cognate immodesties are abuses that right-minded people reprobate, wherever and whenever they exist.' In defence of his argument, Archbishop McQuaid drew on the words of Pope Pius XI, who insisted that, 'in athletic sports and exercises, wherein the Christian modesty of girls must be, in a special way, safeguarded, it is supremely unbecoming that they flaunt themselves and display themselves before the eyes of all.'[28] From the 1970s, a separate race was held for female participants at Islandbridge, and in 1991 women were finally permitted to attempt the same city centre challenge as men, with Siobhán Hoare winning the first women's Liffey Swim in the heart of the city.

Only a global pandemic could bring a temporary halt to the Liffey Swim. In 2021, however, the swim returned, racing up the river and taking a shorter course for the first time in its history. Some pondered if this made the race easier, but the organisers disagreed: 'You can't just rock up and do the Liffey. For anyone with a pair of speedos this is our All-Ireland final.'[29]

Taking us from the Liberties to the Liffey, Watling Street is much more than the sidewall of a brewery, though there is no denying the impact of that power-house of industry on it and the area more broadly. The Guinness Men of old have been replaced by the Diageo People, and modernisation has impacted on the scale of the workforce, but Guinness has been one constant in an area that has witnessed massive change.

3

Fishamble Street

Hoarding at Fishamble Street during the construction of the Civic
Offices (Courtesy of Dublin City Library and Archive)

Just after noon yesterday as the huge throng of Wood Quay protestors reached the shadows of Christchurch at the top of Lord Edward Street, the bells of the ancient cathedral boomed out solemnly and crisply as they have done for centuries ... Around the frustratingly high red and white hoarding that totally obscures the controversial site, the motley throng wound downhill through Fishamble Street, westwards along the quays, and then uphill again through Winetavern Street to the junction with Christchurch and St. Michael's Hill.[1]

The march to save Wood Quay in September 1978 was not the largest demonstration to wind its way through the city in the 1970s, an honour which belongs to the PAYE taxation demonstration of the following year. There was, admittedly, much to march about in the city. Still, the highpoint of the Save Wood Quay campaign remains a demonstration of enormous importance, motivated not by economic concerns but by a desire to save heritage.

As a young undergraduate history student in what was then NUI Maynooth, and with little sense yet that I would attempt to make a life as a historian, I was captivated by the lectures of John Bradley, archaeologist and historian. At the time of his passing in 2014, an obituary recalled him as, 'the first and foremost Irish medieval archaeologist, urban historian, raconteur, font of knowledge on literature, film, chess, opera and so many other subjects. A Kilkenny man par excellence, and a great loss to archaeology and life.'[2]

To my teenage mind, history began in a burning post office in April 1916, but Bradley transfixed us with stories of the battle to save Wood Quay and Dublin's Viking and medieval heritage. He knew the story well, for he had played his part in the demonstrations and occupations. Here was a story that included names like poet Thomas Kinsella, Senator Mary Robinson and James Plunkett of *Strumpet City* fame. These were all public people, who in some cases had gone so far as to occupy the site of the proposed Civic Offices, drawing attention to the rich archaeology of Dublin's earliest streets.

Bradley brought Viking Dublin to life, making it seem tangible and real. The Vikings, archaeology had uncovered, lived varied lives that went beyond any image of the pillaging Dane. Instead, he painted a picture of a developing, living town which was a fusion of Irish and Viking blood and custom: Hiberno-Norse.

After all, Fishamble Street, curving down towards the Liffey, can lay claim to being one of the oldest streets in the capital. The shape of the street is not a modern intervention; all housing plots discovered by the archaeological digs of the 1970s were 'laid out to front exactly the curve of present-day Fishamble Street'.[3] The name derives from Fish Shambles, or fish markets, linking it to the economic history of a much earlier Dublin, and one with which we have a curious relationship.

Many cities have foundation myths – Dublin's is 988. In 1988, a lavish 'Millennium' celebration in the city marked the anniversary of the establishment of Viking Dublin, or at least that was the initial line. Historians of the Viking age pointed to 841 – outside any respectable margin of error – as the year in which the Vikings established their longphort (or ship port) at the point where the Liffey and Poddle rivers met, the *Dubh Linn*. Other moments in the history of the city were suggested as the foundation year of the city, but the theme of 1988 remained a celebration of the Viking town that became a metropolis. One city official thought little of the pedantic historians:

> You can never get these people to agree anyway. After all, there are some who say St. Patrick never existed, but that doesn't get rid of March 17th. And who picked December 25th as Christ's birthday? Nobody was sure what the real day was, so they had to pick something.[4]

Others more correctly pinpointed a moment of paralysis as the catalyst for a celebration of Dublin. Readers of one American magazine were informed that:

> Dublin had steadily declined to the point that some critics described it as no more than a backwater. The birthday party gave the area's one million residents

something to celebrate—and renewed calls to halt further neglect of the city's past.[5]

The year of celebration was a general success, still fondly remembered in the city, with new monuments added to the streetscape, including Jeanne Rynhart's *Molly Malone* and *Meeting Place* by Jackie McKenna, depicting two female shoppers in conversation on Liffey Street.

Even if the Viking longphort of 841 rather than 988 marked their actual arrival, permanence proved challenging in that first century. In the face of native opposition, the Vikings fled in 902, *The Annals of Ulster* describing their flight beautifully:

> The heathens were driven from Ireland, i.e. from the fortress of Áth Cliath, by Mael Finnia son of Flannacán with the men of Brega and by Cerball son of Muiricán, with the Laigin; and they abandoned a good number of their ships, and escaped half dead after they had been wounded and broken.[6]

From 917, a Viking Dublin was re-established. By the mid-tenth century, the Viking was largely assimilated into Irish society. So while 1988 may not have appropriately commemorated these events in time, it was damn good fun:

> The Vikings returned to Dublin last month. About 70 Norwegians and Danes, descendants of the fierce

Norsemen who founded the Irish capital more than 1,000 years ago, rowed replicas of Viking longboats up the muddy River Liffey into the heart of the city. There, they landed and staged a mock battle with local defenders as thousands of cheering Dubliners looked on.[7]

That such an exercise in Professional Dublinism came about in the late 1980s was interesting, coming less than a decade after the showdown at Wood Quay and Fishamble Street concerning the Civic Offices.

★★★

That new Civic Offices had been needed was not a debate; in the words of Anngret Simms of the Friends of Medieval Dublin:

> The struggle is about the preservation of the origins of our town for this and future generations. The Civic Offices must be built without delay. The Corporation employees are entitled to better accommodation. But there are alternative sites for their offices. There is only one Wood Quay.[8]

From the late 1940s onwards, Fishamble Street and its surroundings had been identified as the location for new such offices by the Corporation itself. The hope was that 'Dublin Corporation's scattered collection of office buildings may shortly be replaced by new central offices … bounded by Winetavern Street, Wood Quay, Fishamble Street and John's Lane East.'[9]

For the Corporation, the question was how to bring a 2,000-strong administrative staff into one working environment. Wood Quay was, admittedly, not the perfect site. In 1955 the *Irish Press* reported that 'they had searched the city in vain for another central site for the new offices.' While some suggested sites beyond the city centre, 'that was ruled out immediately as the public could not be expected to go out there to pay their rates, tax their motor vehicles and transact other necessary business.'[10] Whatever of the bogeyman of local bureaucracy in the mid-twentieth century, it

A view of Fishamble Street before the Civic Offices. This view shows Mallin Hall. (Courtesy of Dublin City Library and Archive)

1 Henrietta Street

John Opie's 1797 painting of Mary Wollstonecraft
(Courtesy of New York Public Library)

Henrietta House today (Luke Fallon)

Uinseann MacEoin plaques
on 5 Henrietta Street
(Luke Fallon)

Three Castles Burning:
Detail in a streetlight
(Luke Fallon)

2 Watling Street

Emmet Buildings, designed by Herbert George Simms
(Luke Fallon)

Bonded stores of Roe's Distillery, Watling Street (Luke Fallon)

3 Fishamble Street

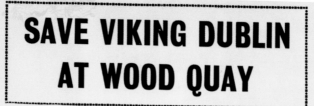

SAVE VIKING DUBLIN AT WOOD QUAY

Campaign sticker calling for the preservation of
Viking Dublin

The 1988 Millennium celebration castles, everywhere present in
the city and still widely found (2020 redesign by Paul Guinan)

The construction of the Civic Offices
(Courtesy of Dublin City Library and Archive)

A plaque on Fishamble Street documenting the archaeological
finds (Luke Fallon)

A gathering on Fishamble Street to commemorate Handel's *Messiah* (Courtesy of Dublin City Library and Archive)

26 Fishamble Street (Luke Fallon)

4 Rathmines Road Lower

Rathmines Town Hall (Luke Fallon)

Kodak House (Luke Fallon)

A plaque commemorating Sheehy-Skeffington (Courtesy of Luke Fallon)

Shamrock detail in a Rathmines street light (Luke Fallon)

should be noted that the celebrated urban planner Patrick Abercrombie, author of the ambitious 1922 vision *Dublin of the Future,* had also earlier pondered Wood Quay and Liffeyside as a site for Civic buildings.[11]

After a debacle around the first approved design, that of the Jones and Kelly architectural firm in the 1950s, the 1970s brought approval for a new plan by architect Sam Stephenson. The son of Paddy Joe Stephenson, who had been a founding member of the Old Dublin Society (and, more curiously, the Communist Party of Ireland), an early newspaper profile noted that, 'Stephenson loves the city in which he was born and reared and recently decided to move his architectural firm into the Liberties.'[12]

Stephenson's plan for the Civic Offices consisted of four office blocks, though he stressed 'none of the blocks is of a size or height which will dominate the Cathedral in scale of character.'[13] Demonstrating the sense of history bestowed on him, no doubt, he referenced Dublin's greatest architect in a profile interview with the *Sunday Independent* in 1972:

> Sam Stephenson, the man who has designed Dublin's most ambitious building for centuries – the new Civic Offices – enters a room so unobtrusively you scarcely notice him.
>
> Small, slight, with a mop of dark hair and a beard, he talks almost diffidently about the £4 million scheme

59

for which the Minister for Local Government last week gave the go-ahead. So diffidently that even his remark to me that 'this is the biggest opportunity given to an architect since Gandon designed the Custom House' lacked any apparent egotism.[14]

Stephenson's proposal looked different from the Civic Offices we know today in some very significant ways. Firstly, only two of his intended four blocks were constructed, which Dubliners nonetheless came to christen 'the bunkers' owing to their appearance. Secondly, and even more significantly, the Civic Offices we know are in fact comprised of two distinct architectural phases and projects – the second, river-facing scheme was that of Scott Tallon Walker in the early 1990s.

While archaeologists were in place at the Wood Quay site before the construction of the Civic Offices began, there was a sense that their work was being rushed, leading eminent British archaeologists to write to Taoiseach Jack Lynch, outlining a belief that 'this excavation is of European importance yielding results unparalleled elsewhere.'[15] Similarly, Henrik Jansen of the Museum of Svendborg wrote to Dublin Corporation insisting that 'the City Council of Dublin has an obligation to northern European culture to preserve it. It is not only a national monument – it is a real international monument which will draw a lot of people from Europe in coming years.'[16] There were critics too, and sometimes from surprising quarters. Professor Michael J. Kelly of University College Cork's Department of Archaeology was of the view that money spent on other sites of interest would give a vastly better view of medieval Ireland, pondering how 'this hole in Dublin' had become the epicentre of Irish archaeology.[17] What other sites didn't have, campaigners would retort, was the imminent risk of construction. Kelly's comments were made in a courtroom, a frequent location for debate on Wood Quay's future as campaigners sought injunctions to allow archaeological work to continue.

What was being revealed on Fishamble Street especially were the layers of Dublin's development. The image of the Viking grabbed the public imagination, and fiery Vikings were the perfect material for protest posters, but the archaeologist Breandán Ó Ríordáin and his team were revealing much of the Anglo-Norman city too, which had grown after the fall of Dublin to the Normans in 1170, and changed many aspects of life for the inhabitants of streets like Fishamble Street. It became, one writer of the Wood Quay saga tells us, 'daily clearer how the development-minded Normans had envisioned their Dublin.'[18] What became apparent in the Fishamble Street discoveries was the continuity of plots, 'indicative of a high level of organisation and collective planning.' Here, it was argued, was some of the earliest town planning on the island of Ireland.[19]

As more and more was revealed, public anxiety grew around the question of rushed development. The campaign not merely marched, but utilised the tactic of occupation, seizing the site in June 1979 and holding it for a number of weeks, drawing more international attention. Academic historian, Augustinian friar and prolific author F. X. Martin was the guiding light of the occupation, but it also included 'an alderman in his robes, well known writers, politicians and trade union leaders'. Mary Lavin, James Plunkett, Gemma Hussey and Thomas Kinsella were present, Kinsella capturing the spirit of the occupation in his poem 'Night Conference, 6 June 1979':

> The high cranes hung in the dark,
> swift hooks and whining spider brains
> locked by our mental force.
> Disturbed pits and drains trickled with unease.
>
> Where were they, with their talking done,
> looking down from what window, the white cuffed
> marauders, visages of rapine and arrogance,
> stealthy and furious above our circle of firelight?[20]

Codenamed Operation Sitric, in honour of Dublin's former Viking ruler, Sigtrygg Silkbeard, the occupiers raised a flag over the site. This was not the tricolour, or the three burning castles of the city, but a black raven flag, incorporating an old Viking symbol. A nun, a priest, several poets, the chairman of the Liberties Association and others all participated in the event. The Danes came as friends and not foes, with the First Secretary of the Danish Embassy and a number of Danes who lived in the city amongst the first to visit the protest. The atmosphere was jovial, the food good enough that, 'one Garda telephoned home and pleaded overtime duties.'[21]

The campaign certainly influenced the local elections of that same month. Lord Mayor Paddy Belton, an unapologetic supporter of the Civic Offices proposal, lost his seat, acknowledging that the defeat was in no small part shaped by Wood Quay. Sarcastic graffiti had appeared on the Fishamble Street hoardings days earlier read:

Congratulations!
P. BELTON
WINNER – 1979
OLIVER CROMWELL AWARD
CONTRIBUTION TO IRISH HERITAGE.[22]

Local elections returned a solid majority of candidates who had committed to fighting for Wood Quay, though as Bradley noted, 'each attempt to take effective action resulted in a head-on collision with a bureaucratic wall.'[23]

A walk down Fishamble Street today, from Christchurch Cathedral and the intersection with Lord Edward Street, reveals that the campaign to 'Save Wood Quay' was not a successful one. Despite that, it is wrong to categorise this street merely as the site of a defeat.

Amidst the controversy, one of the most significant archaeological digs in European history was undertaken. Pat Wallace, later Director of the National Museum of Ireland, served as chief archaeologist on the digs, which revealed so much of what lay below Fishamble Street in particular. He maintains:

> We know more about Dublin around the year 1000 than we do of almost any other European town of the time, London and Paris included. Building foundations of the era of Brian Boru were unearthed in their dozens. The earthen defensive embankments behind which Brian's rival, Sitric the King of Dublin, and his men allegedly crouched during the Battle of Clontarf were revealed. So was the later 11th-century town wall and the wooden docksides of the Anglo-Normans. Nine waterfronts altogether.[24]

The people who lived on Fishamble Street in Viking and medieval times did more than sell and consume fish; Pat Wallace noted that, 'the finds from Fishamble Street have been invaluable in providing information on the crafts and skills practised in the Viking town as well as contacts with other countries through trade. Domestic artefacts belonging to coopers, turners, shipwrights, blacksmiths and carvers were recovered.'[25] A series of plaques in the ground on Fishamble Street and its neighbouring streets captures this diversity, depicting artefacts uncovered during the work at the site.

★★★

Beyond its Viking and medieval heritage, Fishamble Street claims international importance as the street where George Frederic Handel's oratorio *Messiah* was first performed on 13 April 1742, a date on which Dubliners now gather annually on the street to hear it again.

Handel performed in the New Musick Hall, opened in 1741. Then, Fishamble Street was fashionable and prestigious, something which seemed far distanced to a writer just a century later, in a historic account of the *Messiah* published to mark its centenary:

> One would never guess, looking at this old street, that it was once the festive resort of the wealthy and refined. It needs an effort of imagination to conceive of it as having ever witnessed the gay throng of fashion and aristocracy – the Viceregal cortege – ladies in hoops and feathers; and 'white-gloved beaux' in bag, and swords, and chapeau; with scores of liveried footmen and pages; and the press of coaches, and chariots, and sedan-chairs. Yet such was the scene often presented here in the eighteenth century.[26]

Not everyone in the eighteenth-century city was of the aristocracy, of course. In a sense, it was the poverty of a large section of society which directly brought Handel to the city. Brutal winters had befallen Ireland, sending the Great Frost. There was massive inflation in the cost of food in the city during 1740 and 1741, while in the countryside the extreme coldness killed cattle and sheep, creating a supply crisis. Food riots followed, Jonathan Bardon describing how on one occasion, 'the mob roamed out of the city to seize meal from mills in Harold's Cross and its neighbourhood. As they attempted to restore order, soldiers called out from the Royal Barracks killed several rioters.'[27]

What has this to do with the fashionable George Frideric Handel, Baroque composer beloved of the London established and then internationally regarded for his operas? Amidst the economic turmoil that flowed from the crisis of extreme conditions, debtors' prisons began to fill with those who could not pay their creditors. These were not necessarily those at the bottom of society, who were often spoken of with contempt, but included 'shopkeepers, tavern proprietors, farmers, drovers and artisans'.[28] Amongst the bodies which intended to open the gates of Dublin's debtor's prisons was the Charitable Musical Society. This body invited Handel to the Irish capital. Non-sectarian, and open to Catholics, 'its members ranged from titled gentlemen to humble artisans.'[29]

A member, keen to capture its diversity, penned a poem which described the unique nature of the

Charitable Musical Society. It included the words:

> For tradesmen there gave no offence,
> When blessed with manners or good sense;
> Some gentlemen, some lords and squires,
> Some Whigs, and Tories, and Highflyers;
> There Papists, Protestants, Dissenters;
> Sit cheek by jole, at all adventures,
> And thus united did agree
> To make up one Society.
> That some drink jill, and others beer
> Was all the schism they had to fear.[30]

Handel accepted an invitation to the city, with the Society requesting a benefit performance towards the worsening crisis of debt in the city. The New Musick Hall, sometimes known as Neal's Musick Hall (after John Neal of the body), was set as the venue. As it could host some 600 people comfortably, it was seen to have tremendous potential as a space for charitable fundraising. This decision by the society to invite Handel would change the course of musical history for Dublin and the world.

Handel's presence in Dublin brought with it real excitement, the *Dublin News-Letter* of 10 April reporting that:

> Yesterday Morning, at the Musick Hall ... there was a publick Rehearsal of the Messiah, Mr. Handel's new sacred Oratorio, which in the

opinion of the best Judges, far surpasses anything
of that Nature, which has been performed in this
or any other Kingdom. The elegant Entertainment
was conducted in the most regular Manner, and
to the entire satisfaction of the most crowded and
polite Assembly.[31]

Messiah utilised the choirs of both Christchurch Cathedral
and St Patrick's Cathedral, despite the strident opposition
of the ageing Dean Jonathan Swift, who regarded 'a club
of fiddlers in Fishamble Street' as no fitting venue for the
choir of his personal kingdom. It was an unusual act of
opposition from a figure so synonymous with charitable
good, though Swift's mental health was in a state of dete-
rioration, leading to such public confrontational moments.
Even Swift was powerless to silence Handel.

It may seem peculiar now that the site of Handel's
Messiah's debut could be lost, but theatres, music halls
and other centres of entertainment would prove to be
amongst the most precarious buildings in the city from
the Georgian age onwards. Sometimes this reflected issues
in their own stability – like in February 1782, when there
was tragedy at the grove room of the venue when its main
beam, which was rotten, gave way. At least eleven lives
were lost as a result of injuries sustained in the collapse.

The name of Kennan & Sons, long-standing iron-
mongers in the city, would come to adorn the site of
the Music Hall from the 1860s, remaining there into

The site of the performance, later Kennan & Sons (Courtesy of Dublin City Library and Archive)

the living memory of the city. The distinctive archway entrance of the Music Hall is the only surviving part of the original structure. Máire Kennedy has noted that this was a factor in the decline of the venue, but there were others at play too. Across the river, 'the popularity of the entertainments held at the Rotunda had begun to rival those of the Music Hall. This factor, in addition to the accident, led to the rapid decline in the use of the Music Hall for public assemblies.'[32]

★★★

Beyond an archway of a Music Hall, Fishamble Street maintains other features of great architectural significance, though some are not as immediately obvious. 26 Fishamble Street, on the intersection with Essex Street West, stands proudly as one of the oldest houses in Dublin, especially within what would have been the walled city. It has stood there in some form or another since the 1600s. Michael Casey, resident of the house, explained to the *Dublin Inquirer,* that 'the house was rebuilt in 1721, and the outer shell today was built in the 1850s by my great-great-grandfather.'[33] This house played an important role in the battle for Wood Quay, when the occupation of the site in 1979 captivated the city and grabbed international headlines. Thomas Farrel Heffernan, an American professor who would make several research trips to Dublin to tell the story of *Operation Sitric in Wood Quay: The Clash over Dublin's Viking Past*, wrote of how, 'the vantage point from which John Bradley waved a tea towel as a signal to the first occupiers was the fourth floor of the Casey house on Fishamble Street.'[34]

Fishamble Street is a street on which it is impossible not to think of history, even the most casual stroller staring at their shoes will notice the curious plaques in the ground honouring the archaeological digs of the 1970s. It is undoubtedly time to study how history has viewed Sam Stephenson, referred to as the 'enfant terrible of Irish modernist architecture'.[35] In an *Irish Times* poll of 1991, when Wood Quay was still fresh in the memory, readers were asked to identify the best and worst buildings in Ireland. While the top three 'worst' buildings, by public sentiment anyway, were the work of Stephenson (the offices of the Electricity Supply Board at Fitzwilliam Street, the Central Bank and the Civic Offices), one of these same buildings was also ranked amongst the five 'best'.[36]

To my mind, Stephenson's buildings – the chief protagonist in bringing brutalism and modernism to Dublin – are an important part of the built heritage of the city, placing the architecture of the second half of the twentieth century in the story of the city. Alas, if only they had been built at less contested sites, we could appreciate them more fully. In a city where the ages so often sit alongside one another, Stephenson's buildings are still defined by *where* he built, and not what he built.

It is not the Viking age then, but contemporary architecture that Fishamble Street chiefly calls to mind today, even if in other ways, like its curve towards the Liffey, it has changed remarkably little. The protest chants for the heart and soul of the city may now be a fading memory, but there remains a beautiful continuity in other events, like the annual gathering on the street to hear *Messiah* once more.

4

Rathmines Road Lower

> The furniture van was gone and I remember standing in the hallway of the empty house with a small green vase in my hands. I noticed that the wallpaper was cleaner in those places which had been covered by pictures. At that moment the Rathmines Town Hall clock rang out and I nearly let the vase fall. It was the first and the last time I heard it strike.[1]

These words are the recollections of Edward Thomas, son of the Rathmines Fire Brigade Chief James Heather Thomas, of the passing of his father in 1932. In time, Edward would become Éamonn MacThomáis, a popular historian who opened the eyes of so many to the rich history of the Irish capital in the second half of the twentieth century. MacThomáis will forever be synonymous with the pioneering Irish television maker David

Shaw-Smith, responsible not only for *Hands* (which captured dying traditional crafts) but *Dublin: A Personal View*, a show in which MacThomáis rambled across a rapidly changing built landscape in the early 1970s, encountering Dublin and her people.

MacThomáis, beloved of those same people, was as *Dub-a-lin* as one could be, Shaw-Smith's programme capturing not merely his knowledge but his mannerisms and distinctive voice. It was an accent perhaps not associated in the popular mind with Rathmines, a district that instead recalls the well-heeled lost lady of O'Casey's *The Plough and The Stars*, who stumbles into an insurrection and begs for assistance: 'For Gawd's sake, will one of you kind men show any safe way for me to get to Wrathmines?'[2]

MacThomáis spent his formative childhood in working-class Goldenbridge, following the passing of James Heather Thomas. That there was a distinct Rathmines Fire Brigade to employ Éamonn's father, and that there was a Rathmines Town Hall to ring its bells eternally in his memory when he thought of him, are both part of the broader story of a district that in many ways stood apart from the city.

Rathmines is quintessential Victorian Dublin, defined in our minds by its red-brick architecture and the decorative features of the houses that line its leafy streets. The age of Victoria – which spanned a reign of sixty-three years on the throne (1837–1901) – transformed these islands. Dublin and

73

Rathmines Fire Station (Luke Fallon)

Ireland were transformed by changes in architecture, infrastructure, science, politics and more besides. The advent of
the railway system and the arrival of the steamship ensured
a greater connected society than before. Reflecting on that
age, the republican C. S. Andrews recounted that:

> Dublin was a British city and accepted itself as one.
> Its way of life, its standard of values, its customs
> were identical with those of, say, Birmingham or
> Manchester except to the extent that they were
> modified by one great difference: religion.[3]

Andrews was correct: the changing religious demograph-
ics of the city, and the new powers of Catholics within
it – following Catholic Emancipation in 1829, which,
among other things, allowed Catholics to take positions
within government, including Dublin Corporation – did
set Dublin apart in interesting ways. One way in which
Dublin did not differ from the cities of its neighbouring
island, however, was in the emergence of more rigid class
divisions. Social class usurped the 'orders' and 'estates' of
earlier times, and the rise of the middle class facilitated
new suburbs beyond densely packed cities. Living in such
places carried real social capital. Lara Baker Whelan, in a
study on Victorian class society, tells us:

> That the middle class came into its own in Britain
> in the nineteenth century is well documented, but

> despite its continued consolidation of power and cultural dominance throughout the century, the issue of class identification – who was in, who was out and how one was to know – remained a contested issue, primarily among those who considered themselves 'in'. As membership in the middle class grew throughout the century ... the suburb and its attendant lifestyle came to represent everything that was vital to the middle class's perception of itself.[4]

Stereotypes abound in and of virtually every district in the city; as Fionn Davenport explained it to the Dublin visitor, 'it makes the jokes easier to crack and the prejudices easier to maintain. But the truth is a little more complex.'[5] Rathmines had its working class enclaves, its artisan cottages, its nationalist radicals and more besides. Still, a certain view of Rathmines holds a place in the collective memory of Dublin. Kevin O'Sheil, a judge in the revolutionary Dáil Courts during the War of Independence, recounted that:

> Rathmines ... was a Unionist stronghold all during my student days, and for many years afterwards. When the noisy, electric tram rattled over the Portobello Bridge camel-back, you found yourself in another world, and sensed an indefinitely different atmosphere from that of the city you had just left. The first thing that brought it home to you was the

sprinkling of Union Jacks flying from numbers of the shops, and sometimes even from the tall towers of the conspicuous Town Hall. True, Union Jacks were not rare in the city, particularly in Grafton St. and College Green, but they were generally only flown there on festive occasions such as the King's birthday, Trinity Week … but in Rathmines there were, at all times, a few on display.[6]

This sense of otherness around Rathmines was, at least in significant part, self-created. While the word 'suburb' recalls the estates of Cabra, Crumlin and later Ballyfermot, the story of Dublin suburbia began in Rathmines and its equivalents in the nineteenth century, when independent townships were first established. These represented not merely a flight of wealth and influence from the city as it existed between the canals, but the birth of new political entities. Séamas Ó Maitiú, born in Rathmines and the foremost authority on Dublin's Victorian townships, has detailed the way in which Rathmines seized upon a Westminster Towns Improvement Bill, which incorporated 'many previous acts regarding the improvement of roads, public lighting and other matters. This general act was passed in 1847 and consequently any body representing a local area could obtain a local act and adopt all and some of its provisions'.[7] With its own local governmental system, and a wide range of local municipal services, the Rathmines Township was born. Dotted throughout the district of the former township are markers, now a historical curiosity, proclaiming 'Township of Rathmines – 1847'.

Free of City Rates and the influence of Dublin Corporation, the commissioners of this new township instead wielded much power in shaping Rathmines. The first chairman was Frederick Stokes, an English property developer who had developed houses at Portobello (within the city limits) and on Leinster Road in Rathmines. In this respect, Susan Galavan tells us, he was not entirely unique: 'when the Rathmines Township was formed in 1847, at least half of the board members were speculative builders, with the remainder mainly businessmen and professionals.'[8]

What became the most fashionable addresses in Dublin, beyond the canals but still with the benefit of proximity to the city for those with commercial interests in it, began with considerable challenges. Speculative builders may have been at the heart of the project, but they quickly came to understand the importance of good infrastructure in luring would-be residents. No longer within the boundaries of the city, the task of building roads and amenities fell on their shoulders.

There were political issues at play, too, in the decision to leave Dublin Corporation's sphere of influence. Nineteenth-century political reform had ensured a more diverse Corporation, to some a cause of concern. With an emerging Catholic middle class from the time of Catholic Emancipation in 1829, and the gradual breaking of sectarian chains which had kept Catholics from influence in public life, the Corporation and life in the city more broadly was becoming more reflective of Irish life. In 1840 there came the Irish Municipal Reform Act, paving the way for Daniel O'Connell to become the first Catholic Lord Mayor of the city since the reign of James II. When O'Connell had appeared at the window of the City Assembly Rooms in the ceremonial robes of the mayor, he cried out the window, 'boys, do you know me now?'[9] The vociferous cheer from those who had gathered was all the proof needed that Dublin Corporation had changed dramatically and forever. Ó Maitiú tells us the 'nationalist interest was in the ascent since the reform of 1840, and was increasingly represented by small shopkeepers and publicans'.[10]

Crossing over La Touche Bridge, or Portobello Bridge during this period, one entered a new world. Domestic servants would make their way to work over the bridge each day, and so too would the horse-drawn Rathmines omnibus, connecting the city with these fashionable new districts. Whatever of physical connectivity, Dublin city, encircled by its canals, increasingly felt different and disconnected from the new townships which would emerge beyond it. This feeling was commented on, with the Westminster MP T. W. Russell speaking in 1900 of the city and how:

At the end of the last century it had been the home of the nobility and gentry of Ireland. Since then, owing to political changes, there had been a continuous stream of better-class people out of the city and into the townships and suburbs ... the homes of the old nobility were either warehouses, convents or hospitals, and the homes of the better classes who had gone into the suburbs, had been occupied by a class lower, and he could name streets, and especially on the northside of the city, occupied, when he went to Dublin, by mercantile and professional people, which were now poor lodging houses, and in many cases tenements.[11]

The houses of Rathmines Road Lower, though initially sold to that class Russell described so well, are nowadays often subdivided, something we can glean not only from the abundance of bins outside them but the buzzers lined against their doorways denoting individual flats. To later generations, the La Touche Bridge did not mark the beginnings of a township, but the beginnings of 'flatland'. It was perhaps captured best in literature by Maura Laverty, who described Rathmines as having vistas 'of decaying houses given over to boarding houses and flats occupied by poorly-paid clerks, teachers etc'.[12] This road became a rite-of-passage for endless students from 'the country', or rural Ireland.

Even as we approach Rathmines from the city centre, Rathmines Road Lower makes its presence felt
with the imposing domed roof of the Church of Mary
Immaculate. The work of celebrated church architect
Patrick Byrne, the church dates from 1856 and opened
with the spectacle of Dublin's Catholic Archbishop,
sixteen bishops and 200 priests present. Perhaps that
remarkable show of strength was intended to counter the
idea of 'Protestant Rathmines'. By 1876, the Protestant
population of the Rathmines Township stood at forty-
six per cent, almost three times that of the city itself, but
still a minority.[13] There is another way of reading the
numbers; if we exclude the domestic servants recorded –
who were overwhelmingly Catholic, often from within
the canals – Rathmines in fact maintained a Protestant
majority until 1901, the end of the reign of Victoria.[14]

There is a strong surviving mythology around the
dome of the Rathmines church, no doubt inspired
by its grandeur. It feels too lavish for Dublin, perhaps the logic has it, and must have been destined
for somewhere else. As recently as 2020, a newspaper
wrote of how it had been 'intended for a Russian
church in 1917 but the Bolsheviks shut religion
down'.[15] Adding to its origin story, it is also suggested to have been designed and manufactured
on the Clydeside in Glasgow. However, given that
'Lenin had proclaimed that the revolutionary proletariat will succeed in making religion a really private

81

1966 view of the Church of Mary Immaculate (Courtesy of
Dublin City Library and Archive)

affair, so far as the state is concerned', it meant bad
news for Glaswegians in the business of supplying
St Petersburg churches.[16] Alas, the *Freeman's Journal*
reported in December 1923 that, 'the stately dome
designed by the eminent architect, Mr Ralph Byrne
[of Suffolk Street], will soon be completed.'[17]

There may be no connection to the Bolshevik
Revolution, but the church does have a surprising connection to the events of the Irish War of Independence. In

January 1920, a fire rapidly spread through the building, the sacristan arriving to find the switchboard that controlled the electricity ablaze inside the vestry. The Dublin Fire Brigade was called on, for a rare visit beyond the Portobello Bridge into the Rathmines Township. As the flames blazed, Rathmines residents gathered and watched the destruction of a magnificent building.

Others had greater reason to worry. Henry Murray, active in the IRA locally, recalled in his statement to the Bureau of Military History that:

> The Clerk of this Church was at that time a member of 'A' Company and he acted as assistant to the Company Quarter-master. In pursuance of his military duties he utilised some of the vaults in the Church as a 'dump' for the major portion of the Company's arms and equipment.[18]

When the fire broke out, according to Murray, 'there was a miscellaneous assortment of rifles, revolvers, ammunition, hand grenades and military equipment in the vaults.'[19] Murray and others had sometimes slept in the church while evading arrest, a scandal in itself if the news were to break. His comrade, Michael Lynch, had a sense that there was potentially a worse scandal still at play: 'I knew what a disaster it would be to our cause if the British got hold of the fact that we were using the vaults of houses of worship as dumps for arms'.[12]

Rathmines, the only southern constituency outside of Trinity College Dublin that had not elected a nationalist in the General Election of two years previous, was perhaps not the ideal location for a story to break of the IRA hiding guns beneath a church. Still, as Lynch recounted:

> I quickly went on the next day to Captain Myers of the Dublin Fire Brigade, which had assisted in fighting the fire. Captain Myers was a very fine fellow and, from the national point of view, thoroughly sound and reliable in every way. I told him the true story and asked him to see that the Rathmines people got no inkling whatever of the fact that some dozens of rifles and revolvers were lying in the debris under the floor of the church. He told me not to worry, that nobody would ever know. The incident passed unnoticed by anybody.[21]

This was just one remarkable act of collaboration between the IRA and the Dublin Fire Brigade in the midst of the Irish revolution. Later, they would play a significant role in allowing the Custom House fire of May 1921 to burn for ten days, devastating the centre of the British Local Government Board, a fine achievement when one recalls, as Dublin Fire Brigade historian Las Fallon tells us, the Custom House 'was a building then surrounded on two sides by water and on the others by very efficient fire hydrants.'[22] The DFB's role at both the Custom House and the Rathmines fire was demonstrative proof that a revolutionary force depended on the support of other bodies to succeed.

Opposite the impressive church, the other side of Rathmines Road Lower is home to Kodak House, built in 1932. On the intersection with Blackberry Lane, this Art Deco factory is in beautiful contrast with all of its red-brick surroundings, once described as resembling 'a stray project from Miami Beach that found itself cast adrift in Dublin'.[23] There is much about Kodak House that is visually stimulating, photographer Alan John Ainsworth pointing to the 'vertical lines on the tower, the zigzags facing the street, the strong lines leading to the parapet and the ziggurat-type finial: all express-ing the rhythms of "Jazz Modern".'[24] Art Deco recalls the city between the canals, such as the modernist flats of Herbert Simms or the impressive Carlton Cinema of O'Connell Street, but Kodak House is a reminder that Rathmines hosts a number of such gems. Just a short walk from here, the 1934 Rathmines Post Office (formerly the Telephone Exchange) and the recently revamped Stella Cinema are further evidence Art Deco did not stop at the canal.

★★★

Walking the Rathmines Road, soldiers are a noticeable presence in the local community, reflecting the proximity of Cathal Brugha Barracks. Once Portobello Barracks, the appropriately named Military Road takes us to the gates of the barracks, a worthwhile diversion that reveals one of Dublin's saddest memorial plaques. Francis Sheehy-Skeffington, Rathmines resident and social campaigner, was murdered within the grounds of the barracks on 26 April 1916, having gone into Dublin city with the aim of restoring a degree of order and establishing a Citizen's Patrol to oppose the widespread looting. Eileen Costello of the Gaelic League later remembered the sight of 'Skeffy', as Dubliners knew him, amidst the chaos:

> I saw a man speaking to a crowd of people from the top of an empty tram-car near the O'Connell Monument. It was Sheehy Skeffington appealing to the people to be quiet and orderly, to go home quietly, to stay in their homes and to keep the peace. I saw people from the slums breaking [into] and looting a shop. It was Laurence's toy shop. I saw the looters inside the shop throwing out toys and cameras to their friends outside. I felt very great disgust. Later on I saw people in the Gresham Hotel with jewellery they had bought from the looters. I saw a woman with a ring and another with a brooch.[25]

Born Francis Skeffington in County Cavan in December 1873, he had married Hanna Sheehy (daughter of the Home Rule MP, David Sheehy) and taken her surname in a sign of his commitment to the equality of men and women. A pacifist, teetotaller, vegetarian, socialist and more besides, Skeffy was a contemporary of James Joyce at University College Dublin, the names of both occasionally appearing in publications together. It was customary to see Skeffy wearing his VOTES FOR WOMEN badge proudly on his lapel, as he made his way through the streets of Rathmines. He was labelled a crank, but adopted the moniker with pride. A crank, according to Skeffy, was 'a small instrument that makes revolutions'.[26]

The police took an active interest in Skeffy the pacifist. An intelligence policeman, tasked with monitoring a meeting at which he spoke after the outbreak of the First World War, felt it worth noting he 'pointed out at some length the sufferings and discomforts which soldiers had to endure in the trenches at the front, and said that the wounded soldiers who had come home would not advise anybody to go out there'.[27] At the family home, 11 Grosvenor Place in Rathmines, he proudly stuck a Suffrage anti-war poster to the gatepost, which was quickly ripped down by a neighbour of opposing sentiment.[28]

Trying to bring order to the looted streets of Easter Monday may seem like the daydream of an idealist, but Skeffy was dripping in idealism. Arrested by the deranged Captain John Bowen-Colthurst, who was also

87

4.8: A contemporary cartoon, mocking Skeffy (Courtesy of Dublin City Library and Archive)

responsible for the firing squad deaths of two innocent journalists, Skeffy was shot in the barracks on 26 April 1916 for an insurrection he had taken no part in. A brick, containing a bullet which passed through his body, is held today in the collection of the National Museum of Ireland, alongside his VOTES FOR WOMEN badge. Tributes were plentiful, from British Suffragettes and further afield. His friend Padraic Colum would honour him in the pages of American radical newspaper *Mother*

Earth: 'I shall remember Francis Sheehy-Skeffington as the happiest spirit I ever knew. He fought for enlightenment with a sort of angelic courage, austere, gay, uncompromising.'[29]

While Portobello Barracks may have found itself in the relatively sympathetic Rathmines when the War of Independence came a handful of years later, soldiers leaving it and travelling into the city in convoy were still frequently attacked, so much so that the straight road linking it to Dame Street and travelling through Rathmines Road Lower, Camden Street, Wexford Street and Aungier Street was notorious enough for grenade attacks as to be labelled 'The Dardanelles' in Dublin, comparing it to the killing fields of the continental war. In time, both sides demonstrated considerable innovation in the field of the war. Writing of the guerrilla army tactics of the conflict, military historian Joseph McKenna tells us, 'to prevent them from entering the vehicles, the British army trucks were covered in mesh. The IRA responded by attaching fishing hooks to the grenades, which would catch in the mesh and explode.'[30]

★★★

Beyond the dome of the Church of Mary Immaculate stands the former Rathmines Town Hall, designed by the celebrated Belfast architect Sir Thomas Drew. Drew's work includes St Anne's Cathedral in Belfast, the burial place of Edward Carson. Completed in 1899, Rathmines Town Hall was a statement of confidence from the township, complete with its clock tower. To the locals, it is known as 'the four-faced liar', reflecting their own absence of confidence in its time-keeping. Opposite Rathmines Town Hall, Rathmines Library nicely complements it.

Opening in October 1913, Rathmines Library was part of the philanthropic work of Andrew Carnegie, leading Scottish-American industrialist who would give away almost nine-tenths of his fortune in the later years of his life. Carnegie libraries dot the world, from Belgrade to Hokitika, and he received the freedom of many cities for his efforts, including Belfast. There are more than 600 Carnegie libraries in Ireland and Britain, and they appear throughout Dublin's townships. Designed by the Dublin firm Batchelor and Hicks, the style was mock Tudor, keeping it in architectural sympathy with the Town Hall.

It was a curious feature of Carnegie's libraries internationally that they were often found not in working-class districts, but more affluent ones. In Pittsburgh, a city where he had made no small part of his fortune and where his first library project was located, his biographer tells us he 'had no intention of squeezing his new library into a densely populated business district or a run-down working-class neighbourhood. His sights were set instead on the fashionable suburbs in the East

End'.[31] In the United States, many city municipalities 'embraced a two-tiered system of library facilities: a grand central library in a city beautiful setting, and more modest branches erected in working-class neighbour-hoods'.[32] With this in mind, his choice of Rathmines makes complete sense.

In time, Dublin's townships came home, so to speak, as Dublin Corporation successfully extended its boundaries to include them. Rathmines and Rathgar came under the administration of Dublin Corporation once more with the Local Government (Dublin) Act of 1930. There were some voices of local opposition, with a protest meeting in the Town Hall told unifica-tion would be 'taking away from the people all voice and civic administration [and] would destroy local inter-est and patriotism'.[33] By then, there were also murmurs of unease within the township. What had once seemed fresh and new then felt in need of new thinking. Take this letter, appearing in the press mere months before the amalgamation, expressing a sentiment that was then by no means unique:

As a resident in Rathmines, I think the time has arrived when one must ask what the Commissioners are doing for the township. The roads are a disgrace, and if those who are quarrelling as to whom the contrast for repairing the roads should be given to, would take their bicycle or motor cars and drive from

91

> Portobello Bridge to the corner of Orwell Road …
> they must be convinced that it is time something was
> done to repair some of the nasty holes that are in the
> road.[34]

Ó Maitiú notes that, 'the overall mood was that of bow-
ing to the inevitable.'[35] While Rathmines Township may
be no more, there are still little – and big – reminders of
it on streets like Rathmines Road Lower.

5

South William Street

A pub has truly arrived into the consciousness of a city not when it has an established history, but an expandable mythology. The Castle Lounge, better known to the city as Grogan's, sits on the corner of Castle Market and South William Street. In one guidebook to the watering holes of the city, we read:

> During 1973 the notable Dublin barman Paddy O'Brien moved from McDaid's pub in Harry Street and took over the management of Grogan's. Such was O'Brien's reputation and skill as a barman that many of the patrons of McDaid's, such as the writers Brendan Behan, Patrick Kavanagh, Liam O'Flaherty and J. P. Donleavy, moved their patronage to Grogan's and the pub acquired the reputation as a literary pub. The writer Brian

> O'Nolan, writing under the pseudonym Flann
> O'Brien, even mentions the pub in his novel *At
> Swim-Two-Birds.*[1]

Alas, there was very little drinking for Brendan Behan
in 1973, having departed for Glasnevin Cemetery at the
infuriatingly young age of 41 in 1964. Kenneth Allsop,
a journalist who came to know him well, described
how his 'rogue elephantine talent drowned in a whiskey glass'.[2] If Brendan could take any solace in being
dead, it was surely in the fact that his great adversary (or
'wanker poet and peasant' as he preferred to call Patrick
Kavanagh) was also unable to follow Paddy O'Brien to
Grogan's, having died in November 1967. As for the
Grogan's in *At Swim-Too-Birds*? It was, in fact, a different pub entirely, located on the corner of Stephen's
Green and Leeson Street. To Robert Anthony Welch,
that Grogan's was 'a more inebriated Irish version of a
Parisian cafe'.[3] Which, funnily enough, sounds a bit like
the other Grogan's.

In many ways, Grogan's is a perfect institution to high-
light in trying to give a sense of South William Street's
transformation. Once at the heart of Dublin's rag trade, as
clothing manufacturing was known, it was a street without
a strong sense of identity at the time Tommy Smith and
Paddy Kennedy acquired their public house in the 1970s.
They took a chance, a gamble, on what would prove to
be one of the most fashionable streets in the capital within

short decades. Across the street, the drapers Ferrier Pollock & Co listed their stunning home, Powerscourt House, for sale in January 1977. There was some hope the National Museum would acquire it. Alas, as Robert O'Byrne notes in his important history of the Irish Georgian Society, 'in an era of government cutbacks (the museum's own budget that year was severely trimmed) it was not to be and so the building was left to take its chances on the open market.'[4] Some will recall its courtyard not as a centre of fine dining, but a car park.

In James Malton's fine artistic view of Powerscourt House from the 1790s, we see two figures standing to the left – more or less where Grogan's is today – and we are treated to magnificent views of the City Assembly Rooms (now the home of the Irish Georgian Society) and Powerscourt House, now known to the city as Powerscourt Townhouse. The turnaround in fortunes of latter is especially impressive. Built as a Dublin residence for Richard Wingfield, third Viscount Powerscourt, the house was sold in 1807 for £7500. This was £500 less than the cost of constructing it in the early 1770s.[5] That both of these buildings look much the same to our eyes now as they did to Malton is a reminder that while much has changed in terms of the fortunes of South William Street in recent decades, some things have thankfully not changed.

A Malton print was, for quite some time, the equivalent of a risograph print of the Poolbeg chimneys. Every visitor to the city encountered Malton's prints for sale in its book and print shops, and hanging on the walls of its museums. In a paper entitled 'Who was Malton?', read to the Old Dublin Society in the 1960s, P. J. Raftery told his audience:

> The title of this paper, 'Who was Malton?', was prompted by a question asked in a shop in Dublin by an overseas visitor who was examining some Malton prints offered for sale. The proprietor had no information beyond that given in the letter-press on the prints ... To him, and to a great many others, the name Malton was a print, usually coloured, of an old Dublin scene which was rarely identified with the man responsible for the pictures, as master, engraver, and publisher, which have had fluctuating degrees of popularity for over a century and a half.[6]

Malton, as Raftery noted, was 'an Englishman who lived and worked in Dublin towards the close of the eighteenth century'.[7] An architectural draughtsman, we know he made frequent trips to Dublin from at least 1769 and that he worked for a period in the Dublin office of leading architect James Gandon, before being dismissed because, 'he so frequently betrayed all official confidence, and was guilty of so many irregularities.'[8] His depictions of 1790s Dublin are excellent for their hidden layers; as Graham Hickey tells us, 'on the surfaces, James Malton's Dublin is a carefully tailored series of vignettes that presents the Irish capital embellished with the essential tropes of eighteenth-century European urbanism.'[9] On occasion, though, it is everyday life that shines through. There are beggars, unruly dogs, labourers and the occasional wealthy Dub being carried around in a sedan chair.

As for the name of the street, South William Street is not named in honour of King William III, as pondered by C. T. McCready in his late nineteenth-century guide to Dublin street names. McCready's *Dublin Street Names* was a noble attempt at explaining who and what was commemorated in our streetscape. Some of the names have since vanished, and McCready's book is still an invaluable resource, but 'the street was given this name probably soon after the Battle of the Boyne' is a rare miss.[10] It was my own hunch too, in a city where Nassau Street (from the House of Orange-Nassau) honours 'King Billy' to this day. Instead, South William Street is named in honour of developer and brewer William Williams, who laid it out in 1676. The street quickly became a popular residential street, but really came into its own in the Georgian age. Location is everything, and it sat near important institutions like the Parliament on College Green and new emerging streets of shopping and leisure.

Those seeking a sense of the power and importance of the eighteenth-century city will find it in the scale and ambition of the College Green parliament, but standing on South William Street, Powerscourt House gives a similar sense of the city of the elites. A four-storey, nine-bay home like this reminds us that the private houses of parliamentarians in Dublin could be just as impressive in their own way as the House of Parliament. Recall too that this is a 'townhouse', one Richard Wingfield resided in when in the capital. Home was the Powerscourt Estate in Wicklow.

Stepping inside Powerscourt Townhouse today is a visual treat, for it is one of the finest interiors we can freely walk into in the city. The decorative plasterwork and Rococo panels reveal the quality of skilled hands working in the city at the time of its construction.

Continental influences were real, and some of the finest work in the city can be attributed to Italian and other European workers, but there were Irish talents of the first order too. Writing in the 1940s, C. P. Curran challenged the: 'spurious folklore which attaches foreign names at random to so much of our eighteenth century work ... the belief is still widespread that this craft which reached a singular perfection in that century is a thing of sudden growth and was practised solely or mainly by foreigners.'[11]

Within Powerscourt Townhouse we can see the work of Michael Stapleton, born in Dublin in 1747. The son of a plasterer, Stapleton came to prominence as the most talented stuccodore working in the neo-classical style in the city. He was also Catholic, a hindrance to

1950s view of Powerscourt Townhouse (Courtesy of Dublin City Library and Archive)

personal and professional advancement in the life of the Georgian city. Stapleton's faith excluded him from

Georgian decorative features at Powerscourt Townhouse (Courtesy of Dublin City Library and Archive)

the Dublin Guilds, which had much power over artisan work in the city, for most of the century. Despite this, Stapleton's work is also visible in Belvedere House and the Trinity College examination hall. In the hallway and stairs of Powerscourt Townhouse, there is also work by James McCullagh, another distinguished talent of the eighteenth–century city.

Powerscourt Townhouse today hosts a number of small Irish clothing retailers and manufacturers, which in a minor way goes towards restoring one of South

William Street's historic functions. The proximity of the street to Grafton Street was one factor in why clothing manufacturing prospered there for so long. The most famous connection between the two was Jack Clarke's Grafton Street business, Richard Alan, which opened in 1935. Clarke ran a manufacturing business on South William Street, and a fashionable retail unit at Grafton Street. Sybil Connolly, the defining Irish designer of the twentieth century who would dress Jacqueline Kennedy, worked in Clarke's shop in the years of the Second World War, before Clarke invited her to design for the brand. It's difficult today to imagine a time when clothing constantly made its way from one street to the other, and so much of what we wore was *Déanta i nÉirinn,* meaning 'Made in Ireland.'

Malton set out to show us the Powerscourt home in his iconic print of the street, but our eyes are also drawn to the City Assembly House beside it, with a retail premises at street level marked 'Fruit Warehouse'. Art historian Kathryn Milligan, who has dissected this view in a recent study of Malton's Dublin, draws our attention to a host of details we could miss in a quick view of the work that focused only on Powerscourt House. Looking at the neighbouring building:

> Here, in a detail that might be easily overlooked, we enter the commercial world of the eighteenth-century city. Adorning the centre of the 'Fruit Warehouse'

window display is a large pineapple, surrounded by smaller, unfortunately indistinguishable, fruits and flowers. Described by Malton as a 'confined, but genteel, private street', this detail also suggests that it is a fashionable one, sustained by a market for luxury goods brought into the city to supply the best tables.[12]

The City Assembly House, built between 1766 and 1771, was constructed for the Society of Artists in Ireland 'with the express aim of promoting the work of Irish artists and providing an academy for the arts'. Then, it was known as the Exhibition Rooms. Its current residents, the Irish Georgian Society, assert that this 'constituted a tremendously advanced initiative as it stood as the first purpose-built public art gallery in either Britain or Ireland and possibly in Europe'.[13]

Malton's view shows us only the corner of the building, where Coppinger Row meets South William Street. In the contemporary city, it is best to view the building from the other side of the street. Recent years have seen significant restoration work on the windows, ironwork and brickwork of the building, which has encouraged the visitor to stop and appreciate it. The three-bay, three-storey building has great contrast between its red brick walls laid in Flemish bond and the granite ashlar ground floor.

Following its life as an art exhibition space, the building came to house Dublin Corporation, in the dramatic nineteenth-century decades that witnessed the ascent of Daniel O'Connell and his movement for repeal of the Act of Union, which sought the restoration of an Irish parliament to Dublin. It was here, on 28 February 1843, that a major three-day debate on the question of Repeal gripped the nation. The Assembly Room, one biographer of O'Connell tells us, 'was originally designed to accommodate one hundred, but, on this occasion, at least five hundred persons were crammed into its narrow precincts.'[14]

Though in his sixties, and after a remarkable public career in politics with longevity beyond many of his contemporaries, O'Connell spoke with passion on the need for Dublin Corporation to endorse the message of Repeal. By a majority of twenty-six, the Corporation stood with O'Connell, who would subsequently address a cheering crowd from the windows, not for the first or last time.

O'Connell represents the constitutional tradition of Irish nationalism, but the City Assembly House has a surprising connection to the revolutionary tradition too. One wonders how O'Connell, a trained barrister, would feel of the Dáil Courts established during the later War of Independence.

As Dáil Éireann encouraged a boycott of the Royal Irish Constabulary and the British judicial system, it was necessary to establish a counter-system of justice. Much like the existing system, the subsequently

An illustration of Daniel O'Connell as Lord Mayor of the city
(National Library of Ireland)

founded Dáil Courts operated at a number of levels, with different sentencing powers. Kevin O'Shiel, a judge in the revolutionary courts and later a High Court judge, recalled that:

> Indeed the position that emerged at the end of that winter of 1919–20 was an extraordinary one, and one that neither the British nor the Dáil Government had anticipated. Here were whole vast areas of the country, cleared of any resident Crown forces or functioning officials of any kind, handed over on a plate, as one might say, to Dáil Éireann, which, although created by more than a million Irish votes, had been proclaimed on September 10, 1919, as an 'illegal association' and 'seditious body'[15]

Asking people to boycott the British justice system was one thing, enforcing an Irish one proved a different matter entirely. The Supreme Court was located in the City Assembly House, and though the declaration of martial law in different jurisdictions and the outlawing of the Dáil Courts posed a hindrance to their functionality from September 1920, the Supreme Court continued to sit on occasion. By the summer of 1920, it was claimed Dáil Courts were operating effectively in twenty-seven counties. Common punishments, historian Marie Coleman has noted, 'included the exclusion of an offender from an area for a period of time, the confiscation of illicit alcohol, the destruction of poitín stills and fines.'[16] Any business that made it to South William Street's Supreme Court was considerably more serious.

From 1952 until 2003, City Assembly House was home to the Dublin Civic Museum, which told the story of the city from its humble Viking beginnings to contemporary times. Quirky items on display included Horatio Nelson's head, from Thomas Kirk's statue, which had taken pride of place on top of what Dubliners popularly knew as Nelson's Pillar. Brought crashing into the streetscape by a republican bomb in March 1966, Dublin's monument to Nelson predated the celebrated Trafalgar Square column. The head is one of few surviving relics. It is now on display in the reading room of the Dublin City Library and Archive on Pearse Street, keeping his one good eye (Nelson lost the other in battle) over researchers.

There was also the Colt .45 of Thomas Dudley, better known in the city as Bang Bang, a beloved street character who roamed the streets in the 1950s staging mock shootouts with his key. Dermot Bolger, who penned a moving play which brought Bang Bang to life through the perfectly cast Pat McGrath, gets to the heart of what made him so special:

> In that fantasy world Dublin became Dodge City, Whitehall merged into Wyoming, Marino became

Missouri and a Dublin bus could be transformed into a stage coach trying to cross the dangerous gorge of Dolphin's Barn Bridge. In Bang Bang's imagination his presence saved the passengers from being attacked by Sioux braves on horseback. He spent hours swinging out of buses, firing imaginary shots to ward off bushwhackers and bandidos lying in wait along the South Circular Road. While many rich and successful public figures from that time are forgotten, this man who led a life of great poverty but also great imagination lives on in songs and stories.[17]

Dublin is now one of few European capitals without a Civic Museum dedicated to telling the story of the city. The Dublin City Library and Archive has given a welcome and welcoming home to the two prized artefacts mentioned above. If a visitor to Pearse Street Library was lucky, they may have encountered library worker Leo Magee, who was a keeper of the flame with regards to the legend of Bang Bang. Just don't ask to hold the key – preservation insists.[18]

South William Street is very much a part of the city of the Georgian eighteenth century, the view of Malton still familiar. The later Edwardian and Victorian ages, which added much decorative flourish to commercial streets like Grafton Street, are less obvious here. There are exceptions, however.

The clearest exception is Castle Market, connecting the street to Drury Street and the South City Markets,

A reminder of the Civic Museum at the City Assembly Rooms
(Luke Fallon)

more commonly known in the city as George's Street
Arcade. The work of the celebrated architectural firm
of Lockwood & Mawson, who transformed the appearance of England's Bradford as the city grew impressively
in industrial strength and importance, the South City
Markets date originally from 1881. One of Dublin's
most ornate Victorian buildings, a walk around its
perimeter, on Drury Street, South Great George's Street,
Fade Street and Exchequer Street, reveals stunning red-
brick turrets and Gothic inspiration. Despite this, there
was considerable hostility in the city to the arcade at the
time of its opening, owing to the use of English material and labour in its construction. In the words of *The*

Irish Builder, it was 'an English enterprise built by English architects and by English labour'.[19]

Thinking of this arcade merely as the central market hall misses the scale and ambition of the structure; architectural authority Christine Casey notes that, 'at 370ft (112.8 metres) the long, red brick and terracotta entrance front falls short of the Custom House river front by a mere 5ft (1.5 metres).'[20] George's Street Arcade is not a defining feature of a city block, it *is* a city block. The red brick buildings of Castle Market were designed with the larger arcade in mind, and they maintain a great sense of symmetry.

Another interesting building is 12–13 South William Street, now home to Peter Mark's hairdressers but constructed in the early twentieth century – as the Victorian age gave way to the Edwardian – to be the headquarters of the Dublin Artisan Dwelling Company. A semi-philanthropic housing body, best known for the fashionable-but-tiny artisan cottages of Stoneybatter, Portobello and Harold's Cross, the DADC Italianate-style headquarters was constructed to designs by Charles H. Ashworth of the company. The son of a builder from Toxteth in Liverpool, Ashworth's artisan cottages were a welcome addition to the city. They primarily benefited skilled labourers who could afford rents that put them beyond the unskilled working class. Using red and yellow brick from Athy or Portmarnock, Ashworth's contribution to housing in

The former headquarters of the Dublin Artisan Dwelling
Company (Luke Fallon)

the city has rightly been commemorated with the naming of Ashworth Place in Harold's Cross. The home of
the DADC is more in line with nearby Castle Market
than its own South William Street surroundings.

Returning to the beginning, Castle Market gives its
name to The Castle Lounge. Few know it by that name,
and it's a curiosity of history (though in no way unique
to a Dublin pub) that the name over the door is that
of a previous owner, Offaly man Joe Grogan. In many
ways, Joe's touch is still visible in Grogan's, the timber
furnishings being his addition. The *Evening Herald* told
readers in 1964 that, 'those who bewail the passing of
timber in favour of plate-glass and chrome will have
their faith in the Dublin pub restored by a visit to the
castle.'[21] Most of Grogan's additions to the pub remain,
though the television (which he mentioned in some
commercial advertisements) has been thankfully lost to
history. Together with Kavanagh's of Prospect Square
beside Glasnevin Cemetery, eternally known as The
Gravediggers, it is one of few pubs in the city continuing to shun unwanted modernity in the lives of drinkers
and conversationalists.

As previously mentioned, it wasn't the absence of a television that made Grogan's, but the presence of Paddy O'Brien.
As Tommy Smith later recounted in *Martello* magazine:

> McDaid's was Paddy's creation, and McDaid's without
> him would have been just like any run-of-the-mill

pub. His tolerance of the bohemian eccentrics who came together under his roof was the key to his success. These included Republicans (retired and active), trade union officials, chronic students, flower sellers from Grafton Street, writers and painters – both the house and artistic variety.[22]

Scooping O'Brien from McDaid's had ensured a ready-made clientele that would migrate from one public house to the other. Tommy, capturing the changing city, recalled how 'they just walked across the former car park where the Westbury Hotel now stands'.[23] In the words of the artist Robert Ballagh, who delivered Tommy's funeral oration, it was akin to 'seagulls following a trawler'.[24]

The Grogan's set included poet and publisher Hayden Murphy, whose influential publication *Broadsheet* gave 15

1970s advertisement for Grogan's

South William Street – Grogan's – as its address for correspondence. While Brendan Behan had not made it from the
age of McDaid's to that of Grogan's, his mother Kathleen
was a regular, enjoying the rare special dispensation of being
allowed to sing on the premises. As poet Críostóir Ó Floinn
tells it, singing was not an option for most:

> Some verses in the good old style
> That tell the truth in rhyme well made
> Remember, though, no songs allowed
> In Grogan's, just like in old McDaid's.[25]

Amidst the wandering regulars there was Liam
O'Flaherty, author of *The Informer* and *The House of
Gold*, the latter the first novel banned by the Irish state
and its over-zealous Censorship of Publications Board
in 1930. From the Aran Islands, O'Flaherty had survived the horror of the First World War and gone on to
join the Communist Party, seizing the Rotunda concert
hall and raising a red flag above it in 1922 with several
hundred members of the unemployed. John Montague
recalled O'Flaherty's 'ice blue eyes smiling or scowling
as the mood took him … Liam was as unpredictable as
the seas of his native Aran'.[26]

A *Sunday World* pub spy review from 1978 seemed
to capture the pub on an especially good day, noting the
presence of Luke Kelly, 'the frizzy, flame-haired balladeer
with the cleverly-contrived look of a morose gargoyle,'

while 'a Trinity College professor was egging on other showbiz heads to give voice to their talents'.[27]

One particularly significant dimension of the pub was the equality of men and women within it, beyond any division of bar and lounge (or pint and half pint) as was still rigidly enforced elsewhere. One visitor to Dublin, as the dust of the Second World War was settling, lamented how 'since women have broken loose and invaded the bars and lounges, it is growing increasingly difficult to find a man's pub in Dublin'.[28] Our visitor longed for public houses occupied only by men, where:

> ... in it the gravest political questions are thrashed out and settled; race-horses and greyhounds are analysed from nose to tail and their ancestors criticised with all the gravity due to such an important subject; history also comes in for its share of debate, and the arts, commerce, trade unionism and hundreds of other subjects of the day form the basis of many a good night's argument.[29]

Photographer and Grogan's regular Dara Gannon, in a piece exploring the pub, has recounted that such idiotic thinking of whom a pub belonged meant nothing at The Castle Lounge:

> My aunts drank in Grogan's back then, which was a feat in itself in Dublin at that time. Women had

been relegated to drinking in Snugs, away from the eyes of society. In the changing world of the '60s and '70s, many lounge bars sprung up and accepted women with the conditions that they had a male chaperone and only drink non-alcoholic beverages, such as Babycham. Grogan's was different; it would serve unaccompanied women. It was a small step, but it was a big change in a city where, until the 1990s, certain bars would still not serve women pints.[30]

Some of those who made the pub in the years after Kennedy and Smith's arrival are captured forever in the stained-glass windows at either end of the bar. The work of artist Katherine Lambe, a recent graduate of the National College of Art and Design at the time of their commissioning, the two depict different sets of regulars: 'The Day People' in the artwork nearest the front door, and 'The Night People' at the far end of the bar. There are a variety of interesting people hidden amidst the faces in both, including actors, artists, Corporation workers, writers, house painters and daytime drinkers.

Nowadays, South William Street is considerably more fashionable than it was when Kennedy and Smith took over Joe Grogan's pub. *Lovin' Dublin* has proclaimed it to be at the heart of 'the Hipster Triangle' and christened it 'without doubt the hippest street in the city'.[31] Such hollow titles can change quickly.

Come what may, however, the impressive buildings captured by James Malton will be there eternally, and so will the late Tommy Smith's pub.

6

Parnell Street East

Parnell Street East, the side of the street running from the intersection with O'Connell Street to Summerhill, was once part of Great Britain Street. Such a name stood little chance of survival in the streetscape post-independence, though Little Britain Street has survived in the markets area of Dublin. Parnell Street is vast, but focusing on this part of the street allows us to tell a story of the modern city, as a place which has been revitalised by migration. To some minds, this is 'Chinatown', though others reject such branding, including some Asian traders and restaurateurs on the street, conscious that it is a much broader story. Google Maps proclaimed it to be already so, though such decisions are not made by tech giants.[1]

Before getting into the contemporary street, Parnell Street's very existence on a map tells us much about the political loyalties of the city. Amidst the scandal of the affair between Katharine O'Shea and Charles Stewart Parnell – the leader of constitutional Irish nationalism – which split the Irish Parliamentary Party in 1890, the majority of his own parliamentarians turned on the man once known as the 'Uncrowned King of Ireland'. To modern understanding, the very scandal seems ludicrous; Katharine's marriage was long over in any meaningful sense. Her husband, Captain William O'Shea, had a distinguished military career behind him and was himself a Member of Parliament. Their romance had long diminished; however, like a lot in Victorian society, appearances mattered as much as reality. She and her husband would appear together in public, a normality that was important to political appearances. As a result, when news of the long-standing adulterous affair became public, immense pressure was brought on Parnell, ultimately leading to his political downfall.

The manner in which the Irish Parliamentary Party, the Home Rule movement, came to tear itself asunder remains a defining moment in Westminster politics. When questions were asked of who was the 'master of the party', Tim Healy, an MP who perhaps forgot just how much he owed to Parnell, retorted, 'Who is the mistress of the party?'[2] That line is well recalled, more forgotten is his claim that Parnell was 'prostituting a seat in Parliament to the interests of his own private intrigue'.[3] Today, Healy's open misogyny is rightly viewed more critically than Parnell's private business.

Parnell was a political maverick, and an unlikely hero of the Irish proletariat, being a landed Protestant at the head of a movement which was driven primarily by the support of the Catholic poor. His funeral procession, in October 1891, was one of the largest in Irish history, bringing some 200,000 people onto the streets. Amongst the endless funeral wreaths was one inscribed 'Murdered by Priests'.[4]

Parnell had succumbed to pneumonia, though a section of Irish society clearly felt that the trauma of the scandal the previous year had played its part. The betrayal of Parnell, by forces clerical and political, left a lasting imprint on the mind of young James Joyce, but moved other writers too. On the day of Parnell's passing came a poem from William Butler Yeats:

Mourn – and then onward, there is no returning
He guides ye from the tomb;
His memory now is a tall pillar burning
Before us in the gloom.[5]

Many abandoned Charles Stewart Parnell, but Dublin remained fiercely loyal. Today, O'Connell Street is bookended by monuments to the two most significant parliamentarians to emerge in nineteenth-century Ireland. From O'Connell Bridge we see John Henry Foley and Thomas Brock's tribute to Daniel O'Connell, harking back to what its committee recalled as the 'soul-stirring days of O'Connell's agitation, and his priceless services to creed and country.'[6] At the other end of the street, near Parnell Street, we encounter the striking tribute to Charles Stewart Parnell by Augustus Saint-Gaudens.

Saint-Gaudens was a truly international artist in every way. The son of a French shoemaker, he was born in Dublin in 1848, raised in New York City, and was later educated in Paris and Rome. This journey shaped his creative output, which has left a lasting imprint on the American sculptural landscape especially. Monuments like *Abraham Lincoln: The Man* in Chicago's Lincoln Park, and the bronze bas-relief *Robert Gould Shaw Memorial* on Boston Common are considered defining, Sidney Kaplan writing of how, 'Saint-Gaudens' galaxy of bronzes, free-standing and relief, manifold in the scope of their portraiture, is a memorable gathering of images that reflect and assess a crucial period of the nation's history and culture.'[7]

'I mean to make the Parnell monument the crowning work of my life,' Saint-Gaudens had told the Irish Parliamentary Party leader, John Redmond. Not only did he regard Parnell as 'one of the most remarkable men of his time', but he wished for the work to be 'in part at least a tribute to the memory of my mother ... A Dublin woman, a fact of which I am proud'.[8]

The journey to a complete statue was not easy: a fire gutted the studio of Saint-Gaudens, destroying almost all of his clay model. Saint-Gaudens was also viciously ill, cancer impacting on his energy and ability to work. He drew on unlikely sources in trying to present Parnell, telling Redmond, 'the greatest assistance I received from any quarter in trying to get a proper likeness of Parnell is from the caricatures of him in the English illustrated papers in the days when every man's hand in England was against him.'[9]

Saint-Gaudens had hoped to see *Parnell* unveiled in Dublin, and hoped it would be 'a work worthy to take rank with Foley's great masterpiece'. In June 1907, 'the bronze *Parnell* began its voyage over the Atlantic.' However, 'six weeks later Saint-Gaudens was dead.'[10]

Parnell remains on his Ashlar granite pillar, having been unveiled in October 1911 by John Redmond MP. Behind him, the monument tells us, 'No man has the right to set a boundary to the onward march of a nation.' Parnell's pursuit of Home Rule for that nation had not succeeded. The onward march would take a very different form in the next generation.

★★★

Kathleen and Thomas J. Clarke could see the Parnell monument if they stood at the door of their newsagents, located at 75A Great Britain Street, a name that survived until the unveiling of the statue. A veteran of struggle, Clarke was just 58 at the time of his execution in 1916, though years of imprisonment had weathered him beyond it. He had given much of his energy to the Irish Republican Brotherhood, better known as the Fenians, a secret oath-bound society committed to the establishment of an Irish Republic by force. They were willing to flirt with Parnellites, but always maintained that the dynamite stick would lead to Irish sovereignty before Westminster parliamentary democracy. A participant in the disastrous Fenian dynamite campaign (a bombing campaign of the 1880s with targets that included *The Times'* newspaper office, the London underground and the London Bridge), Clarke had endured appalling prison conditions. As Richard Kirkland has noted, the dynamite campaign 'proved to be a debilitating campaign for the Fenians', putting some young leading lights behind bars:

> Even by the usual standards of the Victorian penal system, conditions for these prisoners were exceptionally harsh, consisting of an unremitting regime of surveillance and harassment that threatened both the inmates' physical well-being and their sanity.[11]

Clarke, released in 1898, would spend some time in the United States. It was there he married Kathleen Daly, who came from a family rooted in the Fenian tradition. Later becoming the first female Lord Mayor of

Dublin, Kathleen was, in the words of biographer and relation Helen Litton, 'stubborn, energetic and driven by a fierce commitment to a cause, particularly after her husband's death.'[12]

Their little newsagents, which was preceded by another at Amiens Street, carried the name T. S. Ó Cléirigh over the door in Irish script. It became a popular rendezvous point for radicals in the city, and was constantly observed by the intelligence police of the Dublin Metropolitan Police G Division. Clarke, without doubt, is the most referenced individual in their 'Movement of Extremist' files. The intelligence report for just one day, 7 September 1915, gives an idea of the comings and goings:

> With Thomas J. Clarke, 75 Parnell Street: Thomas Byrne from 11.30am to 12 noon. John McGarry for half an hour between 12 and 1pm. C. Colbert for a few minutes at 1pm. George Nicholas, Galway, for a quarter of an hour between 2 and 3 pm. D. Lynch for close on an hour from 3.30pm. William O'Leary Curtis for half an hour between 4 and 5pm. James Murray from 9.30 to 10pm.[13]

Clarke was fully conscious that his shop interested the authorities. Out front, along with the Irish language signage, were posters advertising newspapers like *Irish Freedom*, the publication of the re-emerging Irish

123

Republican Brotherhood. Sidney Czira, who wrote widely on the revolutionary period under the pen name 'John Brennan', recalled her first visit to the shop:

> I knew Tom Clarke very well and often called at his shop for a chat. The first time I saw him was when I went into his shop to buy one of the nationalist papers that were advertised on a billboard outside his shop. I tried to involve him in a conversation by making some remark about national affairs, but he shut up and assumed a real business manner. He obviously thought that I was probably sent by Dublin Castle to extract some information from him.[14]

Clarke's shop, commemorated with a plaque over the convenience shop which now occupies its location, was replaced by other popular meeting places in the revolutionary years that followed his execution. There were new street corners for G Men to try and blend into.

★★★

Almost immediately on walking down Parnell Street East, the presence of recent migration to Ireland is visible. The Shakespeare public house is now The Hop House, a popular Korean bar and restaurant which retains much of the feeling of its former life as a 'local' inner-city pub, though imagine a 'local' playing Korean ballads and offering bulgogi and kimchi over toasties. The beautiful 1940s signage of The Shakespeare remains. While recent times have brought great new life, and new tastes, to Parnell Street, there is a feeling of transience too. Many shops have (loud) temporary signage, something identified as 'visual clutter' in a fascinating survey of the street by Dublin Civic Trust.[15]

Already, we see the issue in labelling this 'Chinatown'. On a random inspection of a few businesses while writing this piece, I met people from China, South Korea, Myanmar, Malaysia, Nigeria, India, Nepal and Vietnam all working amidst the restaurants and food shops that call Parnell Street East home.

1974 image of The Shakespeare (Courtesy of Dublin City Library and Archive)

Initially, in the days of the Celtic Tiger, Parnell Street East was not synonymous with Asian communities, but with migration from Africa. Sebastian Barry's brilliant *The Pride of Parnell Street*, first performed in 2007's Dublin Theatre Festival, is a sometimes comic and sometimes heart-breaking account of a marriage and a time that have both passed. In it, the character Janet introduces herself with the words, 'them days was before the Africans came to Parnell Street.'[16] Some in the press then called the street Little Africa. Still, within a few short years, it had become – in the popular mind – the beginnings of 'Chinatown'.

Most 'Chinatowns' internationally were born of direct economic connection between China, and Chinese workers, and cities. Liverpool's Chinatown, for example, has its origins in the mid-nineteenth century when Chinese sailors working on the Blue Funnel Line – the first direct steamship service between Europe and China – began settling in Liverpool. Slowly a community grew, and by the time of the Second World War, there were some 20,000 Chinese mariners living on Merseyside. Liverpool's Chinatown is complete with bilingual signage and a beautiful Arch, constructed by Shanghai workers, a city twinned with Liverpool. Fittingly, given Liverpool's historic claim to the oldest Chinatown in Europe, it is the tallest such arch on the continent.

But Dublin – and Ireland more broadly – did not have the same historic economic ties to China that existed on the Merseyside. Indeed, Dublin didn't have any. That's something very clearly revealed in the pages of a brilliant historic gem of Dublin guidebooks. In the 1950s, the writer Chiang Yee penned *The Silent Traveller in Dublin*. An illustrator, poet, painter, calligrapher and fantastic observer of the human condition, Chiang Yee wrote a series of travel books, most famously T*he Silent Traveller in London*, which explored places from his own unique viewpoint:

> I am bound to look at things from a different angle, but I have never agreed with people who hold that the various nationalities differ greatly from each other. They may be different superficially, but they eat, drink, sleep, dress, and shelter themselves from the wind and rain in the same way.[17]

In many cities, Chiang Yee wrote of the local Chinese community he encountered, but here, they are totally absent from his account of the 1950s city. They just weren't there.

While there was no Chinese community of note in the Dublin that Chiang Yee visited, there were some Irish men and women who knew China intimately. Hundreds had served as Catholic missionaries in the country from the 1920s through to the mid-1950s. Images survive of young Chinese men holding hurls, and also of young Columban missionaries engaging with a culture far removed from that which they knew at home. Irish Christian missionaries in China experienced the full turbulence of the decades, including the greatest natural disaster of human history: floods in the early 1930s which claimed some two million lives and devastated cities, including Wuhan.

William Wong, chef and businessman behind some of the earliest Chinese restaurants in the Dublin of the late 1950s and early 1960s, told one newspaper that it was the influence of an Irish Dominican Nun that had encouraged him to move his family to Ireland. But these Chinese entrepreneurs, those who gave us the earliest Chinese restaurants in the city, were a tiny community.

Yet it is members of a different community who played no small role in shaping not only this street, but Irish cuisine.

Some 800,000 people left Vietnam from 1974 onwards. Those who fled the war-torn nation were known as the 'Boat People', but their journey to Ireland was different. Small numbers of Vietnamese people ended up in Ireland, one later recalling:

> None of us knew very much about where we were going or even exactly where it was. When we arrived in Dublin Airport we thought it was only a stopping off point. We did not believe that a national airport of a country could be so small.[18]

The Irish state accepted some 200 Vietnamese people from August 1979 onwards, who were to be housed primarily in the James Connolly Memorial Hospital at Blanchardstown, with two spacious ward units converted to housing. Jim Kennedy, an Irish Red Cross veteran of some forty years who had assisted in the rehousing of 3,500 refugees who fled south to escape from sectarian attacks in Northern Ireland, was optimistic, telling the *Sunday Independent* that, 'the food won't be a problem. These people eat rice, pork, chicken, fish, vegetables and all sorts and, of course, they are great tea drinkers'.[19]

Mark Maguire's very interesting thesis – *On the Other Side of the Hyphen: Vietnamese-Irish Identity* – explores this community in Ireland. As Maguire notes in his introduction, it is a story with layers, a story of 'takeaway businesses, achievement in education, family, diaspora and identity.'[20] What Maguire's thesis clearly captured was the desire of a new community to make a go at it – and how the takeaway business was something they particularly seized upon. They were ultimately family-run businesses, with each playing their own part, from taking orders to delivering them. Mobile food trucks – sometimes bearing the names of these new arrivals – began appearing even in Dublin's new 1970s suburban hinterlands. The food, to popular Irish consciousness, became 'Chinese food'.

On Parnell Street East, the brilliant Pho Viet stands testament to that time of incredible endurance, owned as it is by a family who were amongst those original Vietnamese people to settle in the Ireland of 1979. Today, it serves some of the best Vietnamese food in the city, and is a reminder of the diversity of Parnell Street East too.

The decade that brought such turbulence into the lives of those Vietnamese families also had its Irish tragedies. At 5.28 p.m. on 17 May 1974, a bomb erupted on Parnell Street East. Edward O'Neill, whose father was murdered in the blast, later recalled how 'it was just a big ball of flame coming straight towards us, like a great nuclear mushroom cloud whooshing up everything in its path.'[21] One of a series of

1974 image of the aftermath of the Parnell Street bomb (Courtesy of Dublin City Library and Archive)

three no-warning car bombs to detonate in the city within moments of each other, a fourth explosion on the same day in Monaghan contributed towards what was the worst loss of life on any single day of The Troubles. Ann Marie O'Brien, just four and a half months old, died in her pram on Parnell Street. Her parents and sister were killed too, among the eleven lives lost on the street.[22] From a tenement in nearby Lower Gardiner Street, the O'Briens and others killed that day by the Ulster Volunteer Force had committed no crime beyond living in Dublin. Just as for the relations of victims of atrocities in Belfast, Omagh and Derry, there remain more questions than answers around the events of May 1974.

A commemorative plaque, on the ground, marks the spot on Parnell Street where the bomb erupted. All of those murdered are named at a monument on nearby Talbot Street.

Film director Neil Jordan, who had a relative killed in the explosions, provides an account of travelling home on a ferry to attend the funeral. It captures the sense of helplessness, and the bleakness of the broader picture:

> Every passenger was an Irish emigrant coming back to bury an aunt, sister, mother or father. I can still remember a huge, straw haired Dublin woman cursing the country that had sent her jobless to England twenty years before only to draw her back to identify the bunch of remains that had once been her father … the fact that nobody knew who had

131

placed the bomb seemed irrelevant at the time. It was part of the depressing pall of violence that had smothered the North and was now threatening to spread down South.[23]

Today, a fading plaque in the ground placed there by Justice for the Forgotten, a group representing the relatives of those killed on that day, tells us that 'this stone marks the site where the first of three no warning car bomb explosions occurred'. Few will see it walking along the street, yet it represents a defining moment for not only the street but the city.

The Dublin bombings were devastating for Parnell Street East, which was already financially depressed.

Aftermath of the 1974 bombing (Courtesy of Dublin City Library and Archive)

Pinpointing a time of decline is difficult. Ellen Presten, in her sixties when Kevin Kearns interviewed her for 1991's *Dublin Street Life & Lore,* recalled how, 'Me mother and grandmother sold vegetables and fruit and fish on Parnell Street. It used to be great up there years ago. There were loads of street traders there.' She recounted that by the time she was 19,'Parnell Street was starting to die out and there was nothing down there anymore.'[24] Still, this was before its re-emergence as a multicultural hub.

One of the most intriguing businesses on Parnell Street East is Dublin Mouldings, located at number 99. To step inside it is to enter a world of corbels, cornices, niches, plaques and statues. Instantly recognisable is the Lady on the Rock, ubiquitous in windows across working-class Dublin and increasingly recognised within the iconography of the modern city. In 2010, filmmaker Jessie Ward attempted to uncover the history of the statue, in a work that addressed urban myths and various theories around her meaning. Ward noted that, 'people were kind of creating something out of nothing, putting it on this pedestal of significance, when it's just a piece of plaster.'[25] Just a piece of plaster, yes, but a wildly popular one. Dublin's *Venus de Milo*, the mould was acquired in the 1990s by Vincent Doran at Dublin Mouldings. Two red and white chimneys have never struck me as a particularly unique 'Dublin' symbol, much as I like the Poolbeg Generating Station; instead, the Lady on the Rock strikes me as a more uniquely Dublin symbol.

The windows of Dublin Mouldings (Luke Fallon)

Reminders of recent history are plentiful on Parnell Street. The shopfront of Lucky Duffy's remains at 146, once the oldest newsagents in Dublin, predating Thomas J. Clarke's revolutionary shop. Originally opened in 1902, Patricia Duffy spent more than four decades behind the counter before closing in December 2013. It closed in a time of economic recession, Duffy telling a journalist how, 'It's not the same street. I used to open at seven in the morning but I had to stop because you wouldn't see anyone in the shop until nine o'clock because there's nobody going to work.'[26]

Next door, 147 Deli serves great sandwiches (with intriguing specials) in the building that launched D1

Records, an electronic music label born in 1994 which was central to building a revitalised club culture in the city and to shining a spotlight on Irish talent. Now an acclaimed photographer, D1's founder Eamonn Doyle has had work displayed in the National Gallery of Ireland and captures the city and its people, telling the Michael Hoppen Gallery:

> As a long-term resident of Parnell Street in Dublin's north inner city, there was a wealth of photographic subjects on my doorstep. It's an old working class area, now quite multicultural. At times it's edgy and raw and vibrant, while at others, it seems half-sunk in a weary pathos.[27]

Parnell Street East's greatest strength is contained within that observation – it is a meeting of the old and the new, unlike anywhere else in the city.

7

James Joyce Street

Street names reveal much about the identity of any nation. It is a form of commemoration different from plaques and monuments, yes, but one which fulfils much the same purpose. A visitor to what was formerly East Berlin today will still encounter Karl Liebknecht Straße and Paul Robeson Straße, reflecting the heroes of the Deutsche Demokratische Republik in a former world. Other names have disappeared, for example, goodbye Leninplatz.

At home, Sackville Street gave way to O'Connell Street post-independence, a name by which many were already referring to the main thoroughfare of the city since John Henry Foley's impressive memorial of the Liberator was unveiled in 1883. The city ratepayers – with the power to vote down proposals – ensured that not all contemplated name changes in 1920s Dublin succeeded; in the vision of nationalist members of Dublin Corporation, Capel Street could have become Silken Thomas Street, Beresford Place was to be changed to Connolly Place, and Gardiner Row would be transformed into Thomas Ashe Street.[1]

Politics is the primary motivating factor in the changing of street names internationally. The heroes of one society, and one generation, can be the villains of tomorrow. In the heart of Dublin's north inner-city, however, and only a stone's throw from Talbot Street, it was reputation which led to the renaming of an entire network of streets, in an area once known as Monto.

Monto, derived from Montgomery Street, was a red light district of considerable international infamy. Readers of the *Encyclopedia Britannica* in the early twentieth century were informed that, 'Dublin furnishes an exception to the usual practice in the United Kingdom. In that city police permitted open 'houses' confined to one street, but carried on more publicly than even in the south of Europe or in Algeria.'[2] Montgomery Street, Mecklenburgh Street, Mabbot Street, Tyrone Street and other names of the Monto have all faded into history. Even the initial names which replaced them have themselves been replaced. These attempts at whitewashing a district's past have succeeded in doing one thing: mapping the Monto has become incredibly confusing.

There is a special irony in the renaming of James Joyce Street, formerly Mabbot Street, after a client of the Monto, and one who immortalised it in literature. In the pages of *Ulysses*, Monto became Nighttown. Joyce encouraged his readers to imagine:

> the Mabbot Street entrance of nighttown, before which stretches an uncobbled transiding set with skeleton tracks, red and green will-o'-the-wisps and danger signals. Rows of flimsy houses with gaping doors.[3]

It was a streetscape more familiar still to Joyce's contemporary, Oliver St. John Gogarty, who has even left us observations of the district's madams. There was Eliza Mack, who he recounted as having 'a brick–red face, on which avarice was written like a hieroglyphic, and a laugh like a guffaw in hell'.[4] Lamenting the loss of the district decades later, Gogarty's poem 'The Hay Hotel' – named for a late night greasy spoon which had once fed the punters of the Monto – was the type of stuff that never made it past the Censorship of Publications Board:

> Where are the great Kip Bullies gone,
> The bookies and outrageous whores
> Whom we so gaily rode upon
> When youth was mine and youth was yours
> Tyrone Street of the crowded doors
> And Faithful Place so infidel?

It matters little who explores
He'll only find the Hay Hotel.[5]

Standing at the intersection of Talbot Street and James Joyce Street, it is easy to see how this district came to house a red light district. A stone's throw away is the hive of activity that is Connolly Station, formerly Amiens Street train station. Talbot Street brings with it the noise and vibrations of trains that pass over it on the iron railway viaduct. The railway, like Monto, was a nineteenth-century invention. There were also the nearby docks, which brought with them a constant flow of visiting male labour.[6] And, this being Dublin, there was the colonial dimension. Aldborough Barracks at Portland Row ensured a plentiful supply of young soldiers to the area. A political discourse grew around venereal disease, which nationalists linked with the garrison presence in the city. Helena Molony, active with Maud Gonne's women's nationalist body Inghinidhe na hÉireann which emerged in 1900, recounted handing out leaflets warning young Irish women of the risks of getting close to such men:

> The uniformed soldiery were not then the pampered darlings they are today. They were considered (even by the English) good enough to fight, but not fit to mix with civilians in peace time. In Dublin, for instance, they were confined

to one side of O'Connell Street, i.e. the GPO side. No respectable person – man or woman – would dream of walking on that side of the street after twilight.

But many thousands of innocent young country girls, up in Dublin, at domestic service mostly, were dazzled by these handsome and brilliant uniforms, with polite young men with English accents inside them – and dazzled often with disastrous results to themselves, but that is another side of the matter, and we were only concerned with the National political side. These young girls had not the faintest idea of the moral, social, or political implications of their association with the redcoats.[7]

Monto, as Gerry Smyth has maintained in his study of Joyce, thus 'had an extensive, ready-made clientele of sol-diers and sailors looking to avail of its extensive brothel and pub network'.[8] Dublin, it has been maintained, had a considerable population of young women 'who func-tioned lawfully in brothels'.[9] But Monto was not lawful, only tolerated.

At that same intersection, we read in *Ulysses* of how 'a sinister figure leans on plaited legs against O'Beirne's wall, a visage unknown, injected with dark mercury.'[10] Joyce was referring to the treatment of venereal disease, for which mercury was still being utilised. This 'sinister figure' is undoubtedly then a working lady of the district, forewarning Joyce's Leopold Bloom of the dangers within the Monto.

Prostitution existed in all the major urban centres of these islands, but the absence of good quality employment prospects for women – by comparison with a city like Belfast, where linen prospered – played no small role in driving women into prostitution. Belfast had Amelia Street, described as 'notorious for prostitution', but it was little by comparison to what flourished in Dublin.[11] In 1870 there were 3,255 arrests for prostitution in Dublin, by comparison with just 38 in Belfast. In London, the figure stood at 2,163.[12]

The Criminal Law Amendment Act of 1885 allowed for the closure of brothels, and was implemented with gusto across Britain and Ireland. The preceding decade had witnessed growing public anger at the visibility of prostitution on the streets, including in fashionable quarters like Grafton Street. The street was denounced in the 1870s as 'literally swarmed with women of loose character', while one letter writer to the *Freeman's Journal* called for the Dublin Metropolitan Police to 'clean up' Grafton Street:

> Let some half-dozen men of the G Division [Dublin's intelligence police] parade Grafton Street at the hours of four to six. This was found very successful in Sackville Street during last summer, and I have no

> doubt we shall soon be free of these social pests, and
> can again escort our wives and daughters through
> one of our finest streets.[13]

So, were Victorian Dubliners upset by prostitution itself, or were they upset by where it occurred? An 'out of sight and out of mind' mentality was a significant motivating factor in the emergence of what would become the Monto in the early 1880s. At Mecklenburgh Street, Miss Annie Mack ran her brothel from a former tenement at number 85. In time, up to a dozen brothels in the district would be under her stewardship, leading some to call the district not Monto, but Mack's Town.[14] There were less concerned citizens appealing to the press for an end to prostitution when it was removed from the main thoroughfares, but some brought their fight into the district. Members of the Church of Ireland-linked White Cross Vigilance Association felt confident to proclaim 'the greatest possible change now in Dublin compared to former times', a statement revealing their own confidence in their efforts to that point, and even proceeded to take up a house in the Mecklenburgh Street of the late 1880s, from which they would 'bravely emerge each night on lantern patrol to discourage would-be clients'.[15]

There is little room for sentimentality around the Monto and the madams who ran it. Local historian Terry Fagan, raised in the district and with an unrivalled knowledge of it which has led locals to christen him 'Monto Terry', is an oral historian and one of the driving forces behind the North Inner-City Folklore Project. Praised by the Taoiseach in 2000 as a 'resilient part of the city', Terry spent many years interviewing ageing local residents who had recollections of the late Victorian and Edwardian periods. What emerged in the memoirs of local people was a great sympathy for the working girls of Monto, but paints a vivid picture of abusive and exploitative madams. Their capital allowed them to hold sway over not merely their own working girls but the poor of the district. Mary Murphy, born in the district, recounted to Terry:

> The people didn't like the Madams. They made plenty of money from those poor unfortunate girls. Everything we had in our house went into the pawen to help buy food and pay the rent when my father was not working. Some of the Madams lent out money to the people, who had to pay them back double the amount. My mother and father would not go near the Madams for a loan but many a person had to go to them because they were the ones with the money to lend out to the people.[16]

The brothels of Mabbot Street, Mecklenburgh Street and elsewhere in the district are hiding in plain sight in our historic sources. In the Census returns for the early twentieth century we see homes, headed by women, in which several young women are resident but who are not related to one another in any way. In one brothel in the district, the 1911 census takers encountered a Norwegian sailor.[17]

The story of this street is not merely the story of Monto. The work of Fagan and the North Inner-City Folklore Project has sought to champion a more nuanced understanding of this area, including its contributions to the Gaelic Revival and the Irish revolutionary period. A series of commemorative plaques dot the area today, honouring local Volunteers, primarily those who gave their lives in the Rising and subsequent War of Independence. A more forgotten figure, who hailed from a tenement at 39 Mabbot Street, was William Rooney. A formative influence over the revolutionary generation, Rooney was born in October 1873, predating the emergence of the notorious district that would grow literally around that home. Despite hailing from the tenements of the inner-city, Rooney emerged as one of the intellectual guiding lights of cultural nationalism in the late Victorian age in Dublin. His Celtic Literary Society was the first step for many into what was termed 'advance nationalism', a belief in separatism that went beyond Home Rule. Augustine Ingoldsby, likewise active in the Gaelic Revival, recalled that, 'great credit is due to Rooney, [Arthur] Griffith and their followers for keeping up the opposition to the Shoneenism and Union Jackery of the vast majority of the population.'[18]

The vast majority of people, of course, did not engage in whatever Union Jackery may imply – but nor did they speak Irish. The Irish language movement is perhaps something we think of as academic in origin,

Willie Rooney, a creator of the Gaelic Revival
(National Library of Ireland)

recalling Dubhghlas de hÍde, linguist and scholar who would go on to the Irish presidency. The appeal of the language was broader than that, however, with branches of Irish language societies emerging in working men's clubs and working-class districts of the urban centres. Breandán Mac Aodha pondered if the success of such movements, which brought tens of thousands into contact with the language, 'stemmed in part from a reaction to the superficial standards of the Victorian era.'[19] People longed for something authentic and unique. Rooney focused 'above all on proving the historic existence of a distinct Irish culture that had been polluted by English influences carried, primarily, through the English language.'[20] When 6 Harcourt Street opened its doors as Sinn Féin headquarters in the early twentieth century, it was a portrait of Willie Rooney that greeted visitors. The Mabbot Street poet would die at the age of just 27 in May 1901, a victim of the tuberculosis which blighted the lives of the city's working class.

Rooney was a builder of cultural movements, but Mabbot Street contributed its share of other builders and creators. Patrick Byrne, born in 1783, was the foremost church architect of the nineteenth-century city, and worked from 10 Mabbot Street. His work is today found at the Catholic St Audoen's on High Street, the church of St John The Baptist in Blackrock, St Paul's on Arran Quay and elsewhere in the city. Byrne was a pioneer of gothic architecture in the city. Byrne's neighbour at 19

Mabbot Street, John Benjamin Keane, was another distinguished church architect. Another neighbour, Hugh
Henry, was a carpenter and 'one of Gandon's principal
assistants of the building of the Custom House.'[21] This
tradition of makers and creators on the street continued throughout the nineteenth century, even amidst the
decline of the area.

★★★

On the corner of James Joyce Street and Foley Street
(formerly Montgomery Street) is The LAB, the arts
office of Dublin City Council since 2005. Its exterior
includes a plaque marking the site of the public house
of Phil Shanahan. Born in Tipperary's Hollyford in 1874,
Shanahan was a larger-than-life figure who had hurled for
his native county in his youth, before settling into life as
a publican in north-inner-city Dublin. Active in the Irish
Volunteers, Shanahan participated in the Easter Rising
at Jacob's factory. Unsurprisingly, this created difficulties
with his public house licence. Meeting Shanahan left a
deep impression on his legal representative, the Home
Rule MP and barrister Tim Healy:

> I had with me today a solicitor with his client, a
> Dublin publican named Phil Shanahan, whose
> licence is being opposed, and whose house was
> closed by the military because he was in Jacob's
> during Easter week. I was astonished at the type of

man – about 40 years of age, jolly and respectable. He said he 'rose out' to have a 'crack at the English' and seemed not at all concerned at the question of success or failure. He was a Tipperary hurler in the old days. For such a man to join the Rebellion and sacrifice the splendid trade he enjoyed makes one think there are no disinterested nationalists to be found. I thought a publican was the last man in the world to join a Rising![22]

A public house in the Monto offered unique opportunities to the nationalist movement, especially in the aftermath of the failed insurrection. The Mauser rifles carried into battle were mostly lost, and were not of sufficient quality to begin with. As focus turned to reorganising a movement, an Arms Committee was established in the city. Luke Kennedy, a leading member of the Volunteer movement in the city, recalled how:

There was about half a dozen members on this Committee and we procured quite a large number of arms by purchasing them from British military. A lot of British soldiers used to frequent Phil Shanahan's public house and it was there most of the contacts were made.[23]

In the Monto, there were other lures for young soldiers, which brought moments of fortune too. Thomas Pugh, who had fought alongside Shanahan in the Rising, remembered one regular to the pub who was willing to part with guns for the right price:

> Sometimes an Australian fellow would come in, throw a .45 revolver on the counter and put out his hand for a pound. That was a recognised thing.[24]

Phil Shanahan was elected a Member of Parliament in the 1918 General Election, representing the very constituency in which his public house was located, and defeating the sitting MP, the charismatic young publican Alfie Byrne. Later jovially known as the 'Shaking Hand of Dublin', Byrne would hold the office of Lord Mayor on an unrivalled ten occasions, and the posters MAKE SURE OF ALFIE FIRST are still recalled in the city. As his biographer Anne Dolan notes, 'though at odds with the insurgents, he sought to convince Westminster that the rising emanated from the mass discontent of the Dublin poor.'[25] It wasn't enough in this instance, and the Sinn Féin wave carried one publican into political office at the expense of another.

Getting Shanahan over the line was a remarkable achievement against the dynamic Byrne, but by the time of the General Election, participation in the Easter Rising was the springboard of many political careers. Thomas Leahy, a young republican who pounded the doors for Shanahan, remembered that, 'he often reminded his followers he was a soldier and not a politician.'[26]

In the subsequent War of Independence, Shanahan's functioned not merely as a pub but also as a drop-off point for materials. Dan Breen, the larger-than-life Tipperary soldier who had instigated the War of Independence with the Soloheadbeg Ambush in January 1919, remembered how, 'the lady prostitutes used to pinch the guns and ammunition from the Auxiliaries or Tans at night, and then leave them for us at Phil Shanahan's public house. I might add that there was no such thing as payment for these transactions, and any information they had they gave us.'[27]

British intelligence kept a close eye on the public house, describing it as 'a rendezvous for extremists [that] had often been searched'.[28] Despite that knowledge, and the occasional raiding party, the pub still provided a vital link between arms manufacturing in Dublin – where the republican movement ran a number of clandestine grenade and munitions factories – and the fighters waging war in settings like Shanahan's home county.

★★★

The Intelligence policemen were not the only authorities interested in what was happening around streets like Mabbot Street. The Monto could only function with the blind-eye of the authorities, but Sir John Ross, Chief Commissioner of the Dublin Metropolitan Police from 1901, intended to transform the situation, and to bring about the end of the brothels which dominated the area. *In Dublin: The Heart of the City*, an influential 1980s account of the repeated betrayals of the north inner city by planners and authority, Ronan Sheehan detailed the series of events which followed DMP raids into the area:

> He did succeed in closing the flash houses, whose patrons were threatened with exposure. The unfortunate women did not have reputations to lose. They simply moved elsewhere. Many solicited on O'Connell Street, between the General Post Office and the river. This constituted an invasion of middle-class territory and businessmen protested at the effect on the retail trade; respectable citizens were outraged by the scandalous tone the capital's principal street acquired.[29]

The Monto survived to fight another day. Mabbot Street, a few short years later, became Corporation Street, the Corporation's Paving Committee noting its hope that the change of name 'will have the desirable effect of obliterating its evil reputation.'[30] There was also Corporation Buildings, an enormous public housing scheme opened in the early years of the twentieth century, which had tall gates, perhaps intended to separate it and its residents from the immediate surroundings. Corporation Buildings was a tough environment in which to grow up, but one with a strong sense of community. Corporation Street is still the preferred name of many locally, who seemed somewhat perplexed by the sudden arrival of Joyce onto Google Maps.[31]

The eventual pressure to suppress the Monto's brothels came from the Legion of Mary, a Catholic lay organisation founded by civil servant Frank Duff in 1921. The Legion's proactive approach could create tension between itself and the Catholic hierarchy, but Duff was adamant on the need for action.[32] Duff led a series of interventions into the Monto, later describing them in detail:

> For a moment, I did not realise where I was. Then I saw, and I was so intimidated that I actually backed out without uttering a word. My retreat was typical of the attitude to the problem at the time. We were not without constant reminders of the problem and of the menace it afforded.[33]

Securing the support of Garda Commissioner William Murphy, Duff's insistence led to a 1925 police raid which marked a definitive defeat for the madams. Readers of one newspaper, reporting on the dramatic raids, were informed that, 'it is not wise from the point of view of the police that a whole area should be allowed to indulge in the notion that it is immune from interference by the law.'[34] The arrested included forty-five prostitutes, twelve pimps and fifty customers. It says something of the peculiar nature of Irish society then that, 'most of the women involved were subsequently released into the custody of the Legion of Mary and were placed in the Sancta Maria hostel.' Likewise, it says much that Commissioner Murphy's primary motivating factor was that Monto was 'a blot on the reputation of a Catholic city.'[35]

As the police departed, Duff symbolically fixed a large crucifix to a wall, marking the triumph of the Legion. Yet prostitution remained, with streetwalking increasing and new – albeit more scattered – brothels throughout the immediate area.[36]

★★★

A year after the closure of the Monto, Seán O'Casey's *The Plough and the Stars* was performed in the Abbey Theatre, a play that revealed much of the frustrations of the playwright with the Easter Rising and the revolutionary forces behind it. He was furious at what he regarded as the abandonment of socialism by James Connolly and those around him in aligning themselves with the nationalist cause, writing in its immediate aftermath that under Connolly's stewardship, 'Liberty Hall was now no longer the headquarters of the Irish Labour movement, but the centre of Irish National disaffection.'[37] Yet the primary source of discontent with O'Casey's play, which triggered some scenes of protest in the theatre, was the presence of what some viewed as an 'immoral woman' on stage. O'Casey's play utilised Rosie Redmond, a prostitute, who insisted the men were out 'to fight for freedom that wouldn't be worth winnin' in a raffle'.[38] O'Casey found the humour in the comments of one protesting citizen, who told him bluntly that 'I'd like you to know that there isn't a prostitute in Ireland from one end of it to th' other.'[39] Perhaps there was no longer a prostitute on Corporation Street 'from one end of it to th' other', but they remained in every Irish urban centre more broadly, despite what that protesting voice chose to believe.

Song ensured the Monto would not be forgotten. In the 1950s the writer, pianist and composer George Desmond Hodnett – better known as Hoddy – was working in the bohemian Pike Theatre, nestled up Herbert Lane in Ballsbridge. The Pike was important as an opponent of censorship, and a champion of emerging Irish talent, bringing to the stage work by Behan and Beckett amongst others. As a performer in the popular midnight Pike Revue, Hoddy penned 'Take Her Up to Monto', a satire on Irish folk songs, though he saw the irony in how, 'it has become the folk song it originally aimed at satirising.' Sat against the backdrop of the Second Boer War, and Queen Victoria's 1900 visit to the capital, its verses referenced the protagonists of the day (like the feared Boer General De Wet), and encouraged the departing soldiery to make one last visit to the Monto before departure:

5 South William Street

James Malton's view of Powerscourt Townhouse
(Art Institute Chicago)

The stunning red brick turrets of Castle Market, one of Dublin's
most ornate Victorian buildings (Luke Fallon)

A rare view of Daniel O'Connell from 1844. This daguerreotype,
an early form of photography, was taken by Alexander Doussin
Dubreuil (National Gallery of Ireland)

Kathleen Behan painted by Sarah Henrietta Purser
(National Gallery of Ireland)

D'Firm, a fondly recalled regular at Grogan's over many years
(Dara Gannon)

6 Parnell Street East

Michael Walker image of the Parnell statue
(National Library of Ireland)

Thomas J. Clarke stands at the door of his newsagents (National
Library of Ireland)

Plaque to Thomas J. Clarke (Luke Fallon)

A reminder of Lucky Duffy's, once the oldest newsagents in Dublin (Luke Fallon)

7 James Joyce Street

James Joyce (1934) by Jacques-Émile Blanche
(National Gallery of Ireland)

1918 General Election poster for Philip Shanahan
(National Library of Ireland)

Commemorative plaque to Shanahan's public house
(Luke Fallon)

8 Ship Street

1988 image facing onto Ship Street from the steps connecting it to
Castle Street (Courtesy of Dublin City Library and Archive)

Commemorative plaque to Hanna Sheehy-Skeffington (Courtesy
of Dublin City Library and Archive)

A marker showing the route of Dublin's medieval walled defence
(Luke Fallon)

You've seen the Dublin Fusiliers,
The dirty old bamboozeleers,
De Wet'll kill them chiselers, one, two, three.
Marching from the Linen Hall
There's one for every cannonball,
And Vicky's going to send them all, o'er the sea.
But first go up to Monto, Monto, Monto
March them up to Monto, lan-ge-roo,
To you![40]

Today, it is the complex and confusing legacy of the
Monto that seems to draw people into the area and to

A 1971 image from Corporation Street (now James Joyce Street)
looking towards Talbot Street (Courtesy of Dublin City Library
and Archive)

engage with it. There are the walking tours of Terry
Fagan, which reveal the few surviving pieces of the
urban fabric of the area, but which primarily draw on
the rich oral history collections he and his co-workers
have gathered. In 2010 ANU Productions, a site-specific
theatre company that bring challenging and engaging work before audiences across the city of Dublin,
launched *The Monto Cycle*. This series of works enabled
spectators 'to encounter the history, people, geography
and very materiality of the Monto'. It was, like much
of ANU's output, uncomfortable but important work.[41]

The area also hosts unique Bloomsday celebra-
tions each year, with collaborations between groups
like HOPE (Hands on Peer Education) and the North
Inner City Folklore Project. In 2000, at the height of
the Celtic Tiger, one visiting Joycean writing on the city
felt compelled to comment on passing the street that,
'I'm glad I'm on a bus. It feels a bit rough … I get the
feeling the area is definitely trying to move away from
its scandalous heritage'.[42] How much of a feeling can
one get from the upper deck of a passing bus? It perhaps
revealed much broader attitudes in culture, but a visit to
James Joyce Street today reveals many community workers, interested artists and local historians like Terry Fagan
committed to utilising the past in a way that builds pride
in the present and hope in the future.

Much more than a satirical song, Monto was a difficult and dramatic existence, for gun-runners, would-be

reformers and 'working girls' alike. Life on Corporation Street, renamed but still blighted by poverty, was difficult too in newly independent Ireland, but not without its joy and strong sense of community. Reflecting on it in her memoir, *Diamond Memories*, local woman Mary Corbally would remember that, 'everyday was a filled day. It wasn't like *Strumpet City* – it was a great place, more like *The Plough and The Stars*. You were poor but never hungry.'[43]

8

Ship Street

English and Irish language street names are not always in kilter across the island of Ireland. Some peculiar variations in place names reflect earlier colonial rule, something beautifully captured in Brian Friel's 1980 play *Translations*, where a series of phonetic equivalents are imposed on Irish places in defiance of centuries of tradition. This had some curious effects on both languages, as 'a whole new range of English words was created, some of which made little sense except in terms of pronunciation'.[1]

Can regional dialect, and accent, affect the names we see on our city streets? Engine Alley, located in the Liberties, was formerly Indian Alley. Local lore has it that pronunciation played a role in the metamorphosis: imagine the local children in a game of *'cowboys and injuns'*. Similarly, Sráid na gCaorach is a name that has nothing whatsoever to do with ships, instead

translating as Sheep Street. That a medieval name linking the district to an animal would become something
else entirely is likely to owe something to 'the vagaries
of spoken language'.[2]

The name Sheep Street transforms the place of this
street in the history of the capital, placing it alongside
streets like Fishamble Street, Bull Alley and Cornmarket.
It is not shipbuilders or sailors that this street should
evoke, but Dublin's rich culinary history and the role of
animals in the life of the capital.[3]

Animals in the city were not exclusively a medieval
phenomenon. In the Victorian age and after, cows were
frequently kept in the rear yards of tenement blocks, a
source of milk on which poorer Dubliners depended. In
the pages of the *Dublin Journal of Medical Science*, readers were told in 1893 of how, 'there are cow-yards in
Dublin which are a disgrace to the city, and are a source
of danger to its inhabitants … It is almost impossible to
arrive at the exact number of these yards, as many of
them are small enough to be hidden away behind houses
in densely crowded districts, but there are at least over
500 of them.'[4] Inner-city abattoirs, dairy yards and sheep
grazing areas are all no more, but a map of Dublin – in
this case one *as Gaeilge* – can reveal traces of that history.

The story of Ship Street is synonymous with that of
neighbouring Dublin Castle, established by Royal Charter
in 1204. The seat of English and later British rule on the
island of Ireland, it fulfilled a variety of roles as a political,

social and symbolic centre of power, including hosting royal visits, a lavish social calendar, and housing significant parts of British bureaucracy and intelligence work. Double-agent during the War of Independence Ned Broy recounted it as being 'believed by the people to be the centre and focus of all that was evil and secret and sinister'.[5] Not all of the people were separatists of course, and on those deemed too sympathetic to the institution was bestowed a damning term of no endearment: 'Castle Catholic'. There's real disdain in the memoir of Irish political activist and public servant C. S. Andrews, who believed 'an invitation to a garden party at the Viceregal Lodge or to a reception at Dublin Castle was the realisation of their social ambitions'.[6]

Ship Street stood in some contrast to the opulence of the Castle, indeed the Castle was once called 'that bleak fortress situated in the heart of the slums', while the street itself was described by one more accustomed to Castle balls than tenement realities as 'plague spotted, pestilential as a corpse, quick with the life of the worm'.[7]

Not alone is the name of Ship Street muddled by history, there is little agreement on the name of the steps which bring one to it from nearby Castle Street. To the American artist Flora Mitchell, who captured Dublin in a moment of transformation for her study *Vanishing Dublin* in 1966, the steps were 'the dark awe-inspiring flight of steps' she knew as 'Castle Steps'.[8] To others, they are assumed to be the 'Forty Steps', a name also bestowed on Cromwell's Quarters, a series of steps in Kilmainham

An undated photograph of Castle Steps from the collection of
artist William Frazer (National Library of Ireland)

linking Bow Lane and James's Street, and a series of steps
at nearby St Audoen's, amongst other Dublin locations.
None of the passageways has forty steps, but all have a
strong mythology and folklore.

The only ghost which haunts this passageway,
despite what the ghost tours which utilise its unique
atmosphere may suggest, is the ghost of Robert
Emmet's abortive 1803 rebellion. The last sting of
the dying wasp that was the United Irish conspiracy,
Emmet led an attempted rebellion five years on from
the previously unsuccessful rebellion of 1798, though
it never reached the Castle gates as he had hoped.

The fear of that insurrection repeating itself was significant enough that leading architect Francis Johnston was commissioned to design a new protective castle gate on Ship Street and the curtain wall which encloses the castle from Castle Street down to Ship Street itself. The imposing wall, and the steps, date from that 1807 intervention. Maurice Craig, a leading authority on the eighteenth- and nineteenth-century city, regarded Johnston as being, 'after Gandon, the greatest name in Irish architecture.'[9]

His Chapel Royal in the Castle grounds, finished in 1814, is a stunning early example of Gothic revival architecture in the city and reveals much flair, but it was fear that created this wall and passageway. Emmet's rising may have failed in seizing Dublin Castle, but it did transform its appearance – and captured the imagination of later revolutionary generations. A Volunteer would recall the words of Patrick Pearse in the General Post Office (coincidently also designed by Francis Johnston) when insurrection came once more in 1916: 'He pointed out to us that as the dogs lapped up the blood of Robert Emmet in the streets of Dublin in 1803. Dublin was under a sort of disgrace since then. It was now wiped out.'[10]

★★★

Beyond Irish separatists, Dublin Castle had a variety of other political opponents. In June 1912, windows belonging to the Castle at Ship Street were smashed by members of the Irish Women's Franchise League (IWFL), borrowing a tactic from the radical Suffragette movement in England. Windows at the General Post Office, Custom House and Ship Street were smashed to bring attention to the cause of suffrage. Some Irish suffragettes had actively partaken in these activities in Britain, including Marguerite Blanche Palmer, who was sentenced to a week's imprisonment for breaking two windows at the War Office in London in 1911, and who had earlier won some notoriety in Dublin for heckling Edward Carson as he spoke at Rathmines Town Hall. [11]

There was no apology for the action in the pages of *The Irish Citizen*, newspaper of the IWFL. Instead, the women struck a note of defiance, with one insisting, 'I for one refuse to sit down under injustice, and that is why I went out early on Thursday morning and used the time-honoured political weapons – stones.'[12]

Prominent suffragette, Hanna Sheehy-Skeffington, recalled of the Ship Street protest that, 'the policeman who grabbed my arm instinctively seized the right, and as I am left-handed, that gave me a chance to get in a few more panes before the military arrived and my escort led me off.'[13] The women were angry not merely at Dublin Castle, but at constitutional Irish nationalists who sought Home Rule for Ireland without the provision of votes for women. *The Irish Times* deplored 'this childish campaign of window breaking', but the window breaking struck a chord with some. Over 200 supporters attended the court date of the women, with 'the prisoners being handed bouquets of flowers as they were brought into the court room.'[14]

In one of the more eye-catching commemorative events of the Decade of Centenaries, Hanna Sheehy-Skeffington's granddaughter, Dr Micheline Sheehy Skeffington, re-enacted the smashing of the Ship Street windows before an audience which included President Michael D. Higgins in 2018, marking the centenary of the Representation of the People Act which put the vote into the hands of (some) women. In the words of President Higgins, 'one hundred and six years ago, eight brave and distinguished citizens carried out an act of civic disobedience that would have a powerful symbolic significance that resonates down to this day.'[15] It was all far removed from the discourse of the time, which was largely a mix of derision and disgust. No publication devoted more space to mocking the IWFL than the satirical illustrated *The Lepracaun*:

Mary had a little bag
And in it was a hammer
For Mary was a Suffragette
For votes she used to clamour
She broke a pane of glass one day
Like any naughty boy
A constable came along
And now she's in Mountjoy.

If there is a criticism to be made of the plaque commemorating the smashing of the windows, it is that it names just Hanna Sheehy-Skeffington, prioritising the most familiar of the activists. Of the others, convicted specifically for the Ship Street windows, there are some fascinating lesser-known lives. There was 'Margaret Murphy', a *nom de guerre* utilised by Leila Gertrude Garcias de Cadiz, born in India to a Spanish father and a Roscommon-born mother. Cadiz, like her sister

Cartoon from *The Lepracaun* showing a Dublin Metropolitan Policeman leading away a Suffragette (Courtesy of Dublin City Library and Archive)

Rosalind, was a blooded veteran of militant suffrage activism, receiving the 'Hunger Strike Medal' from the Women's Social and Political Union in Britain. She was present at the so-called Black Friday demonstration of November 1910, when London's Metropolitan Police brutally assaulted suffrage protestors in the vicinity of the British Houses of Parliament, leading to the subsequent deaths of two suffragettes.[16] After the horror of Black Friday, widely condemned in the contemporary press and inside the House of Commons, a few broken windows on Ship Street was light work for de Cadiz.

Ship Street is divided into Ship Street Little, which leads towards Bride Street, and Ship Street Great, the larger part of the road that carries a visitor to the intersection with Stephen Street. It is Ship Street Little which provides us with a fine uninterrupted stretch of Dublin's medieval walled defensives, one of the most significant remaining pieces of the wall. From Little Ship Street, it seems a commanding defensive presence, but viewed from the carpark on the other side it is a different matter, with a 2004 Conservation Report maintaining that, 'the private ownership of derelict sites on the northern and southern sides of the wall has left the wall in this location particularly vulnerable and in a state of acute structural instability in one location.'[17]

The walls which once surrounded Dublin are viewed as a symbol of Anglo-Norman triumph, replacing earlier and more primitive Viking and Hiberno-Norse wooden

NOTHING FOR THEIR "PANES."

The Militant Suffragettes (again at work in
Dublin), are by their destructive methods alienating
a lot of sympathy from their cause.

Cartoon from *The Lepracaun* showing a Suffragette smashing windows entitled 'sympathy with the cause' (Courtesy of Dublin City
Library and Archive)

defences. Hiberno-Norse Dublin, a fusion of Viking and native influence, was defended by its own embankments. Patrick Wallace, so central to the excavations of Dublin's Viking archaeological past, tells us that, 'the idea of defending towns within earthen embankments, the predecessors of medieval town walls, was widespread in different parts of northern Europe from the late ninth and early tenth centuries.'[18] The first stone defensive wall for Dublin was constructed in Hiberno-Norse times, beginning around 1100, but the Anglo-Normans later brought new uniformity and technique to the structures, which included sentries.

While the wall has survived the passing of time – at least here – much of the urban landscape around Ship Street has been transformed. Gone without trace is the small alley of Hoey's Court, recalled by a plaque at the Ship Street entrance to the Castle Steps. Hoey's Court itself would likely be forgotten to time were it not for being the (reputed) birthplace in November 1667 of Jonathan Swift, dean of nearby St Patrick's Cathedral and towering satirist. Swift is best recalled for *Gulliver's Travels* (1726), *A Modest Proposal* (1729) and other works which were so defining in impact that powerful political satire is still branded 'Swiftian'. This area of the city honours his legacy in a variety of ways. On neighbouring Bride Street and Golden Lane, a series of eight terracotta plaques on public housing tell the story of Lemuel Gulliver, the fictional protagonist who finds himself in

Lilliput. Swift's head is also depicted on the Chapel Royal within Dublin Castle, the work of sculptors Edward and John Smyth.[19]

Within such a symbol of the political order, the grounds of Dublin Castle, there is some irony in the appearance of Swift, a constant critic of the ruling powers. While *Gulliver's Travels* is the defining work of Swift to our generation, Dubliners of his own time knew him instead from his pamphlets – written under the pen name of The Drapier – which championed Irish manufacturing and decried injustice. As Jonathan Bardon noted, the Drapier, as far as the people of the city were concerned, 'had courageously courted prosecution in defence of the ordinary people of the city … there was hardly a weaver or a maidservant in Dublin who did not know of this clergyman who had so often reached for his corrosive quill to lampoon with savage wit those in power, especially those who attempted to threaten the rights and livelihoods of his fellow citizens.'[20]

Pubs bore the name The Drapier's Head, with signs showing Swift, and his birthday became a day of remarkable celebration. There were bonfires burning to mark the day, fireworks, barrels of ale consumed on the streets. When we think of him walking through the Liberties, it's of a man not merely known to all, but knowing all. As he described it to his friend Alexander Pope:

> I am Lord Mayor of 120 houses, I am absolute lord
> of the greatest cathedral in the Kingdom, I am at
> peace with the neighbouring princes – the Lord
> Mayor of the City and the Archbishop of Dublin;
> only the latter, like the King of France, sometimes
> attempts encroachments on my dominions.[21]

★★★

Not alone is little Hoey's Court gone, so too are other humble streets and alleys which dotted this district, like Cole's Alley, recalled as a 'warren of old houses'.[22] Situated between two cathedrals, and beside the castle, it seems peculiar the area was allowed slip into such urban decay, leading *The Irish Builder* to comment in 1886 that, 'the locality and its offshoots and alleys are filthily dirty and dilapidated … St Patrick's is like the jewel in the toad's head. Could it be transported elsewhere, or could elsewhere be made to surround it, would indeed be a boom.'[23]

Within two decades of that observation, elsewhere *did* begin to surround it. It is difficult to picture this area in the opening years of the last century, when Dubliners knew it as part of 'Little Italy', a district inhabited by Italian migrants to the city. Centred on Werburgh Street, Chancery Street and Little Ship Street, this small but influential community would come to play a role in Dublin's culinary identity, its literature and political life.

Ireland's Italian community at the time of the 1911 census numbered fewer than 400 immigrants, with significant clusters in both Belfast and Dublin. Though numerically small, in the broader picture of the fabric of the respective cities, the manner in which many of the Italian families came to live in just a few small streets in both made them a clear presence.

There were class divisions within the Dublin-based community – one group came from the Lucca region and was 'made up of artisans, plaster workers and woodworkers, with surnames like Bassi, Corrieri, Dehini, Giuliani and Nanetti'. The other contingent, from the Val di Comino, included familiar names like Forte and Fusco and were largely described as 'street-sellers of ice cream or café owners.'[24]

In the latter camp belonged Giuseppe Cervi, a resident of Ship Street who hailed from a small place named Picinisco in the province of Frosinone, and who arrived in Dublin in the late nineteenth century. Cervi is widely credited with opening Dublin's first fish and chip shop, or 'chipper' as they're commonly known in the city. His son, Tony Cervi, recounted that:

> The area around us – off St. Werburgh Street – was known as 'Little Italy'. If someone came to Dublin and wanted to locate a particular Italian, he would more often than not be directed to Little Italy. The place was filled with barrel-organ men, ice-cream

men who travelled the city with their barrows, and with marble men.[25]

Tony remembered the family house on Ship Street as a lodging house which was popular with visiting Italian and Greek terrazzo workers, but also as a place from which Cervi and his wife sold fish and chips, a custom they had begun from a stall on Great Brunswick Street in 1882. Little Ship Street was strictly takeaway. In time, the name of Cervi would adorn a shop there, advertising 'friend fish and chips'. It was from the broken English of Cervi and his wife that a part of Dublin lingo was born, the 'one and one'. As Tony recounted:

> Someone would come into the shop and ask for such a thing ... My father would put up his finger in query. The customer would point to the chips ... one of that, then to the fish ... one of that. So began the familiar phrase![26]

The poet and printer Vincent Caprani, himself a product of Italian migration to Dublin, included Cervi in his poem 'The Dubliner', a work that honoured the many little parts that make up the city, from weavers to soldiers. In their midst, Caprani nodded towards 'the olive-skinned Eye-talian man that invented wan and wan'.[27] Others attributed the phrase to Cervi's wife, who would ask customers, *'uno di questo, uno de quello?'*[28]

There was great vibrancy in how Tony described life on Ship Street and in the surrounding area in the early years of the twentieth century. His father was the 'big man around Little Italy':

> I remember great times when we had a kind of Mardi Gras – especially at Christmas and New Year's Eve. My father would hire out a lot of barrel-organs and get the players to compete with different tunes. The whole district would be filled with music and cheer.[29]

Dublin's Italian community would produce a lord mayor, with Joseph Nannetti reaching the office of First

Cervi's Pearse Street Chipper (Courtesy of Dublin City Library and Archive)

Citizen in 1906. A printer and trade unionist, Joyce includes Nannetti in the pages of *Ulysses*. The son of an Italian sculptor and modeller, Nannetti's roots were in the Tuscan region and his life was considerably more comfortable than that of many of the organ grinders, ice cream vendors and general labourers of Ship Street and its surroundings.

The 1901 and 1911 census returns give us a sense of Dublin's Italian community and their livelihoods, with organ grinders, ice cream vendors and more present. At first, I struggled to find Giuseppe Cervi amidst the community he was at the heart of, before realising he had – not unlike Irish migrants abroad – Anglicised his name, becoming Joseph. The father of the Irish chipper is listed as a 'hawker'.

The Italians of Ship Street were outnumbered by its soldiery, to whom Ship Street Barracks was home. The barracks, housed in buildings purchased by the War Office in 1858, stood in considerable contrast to the tenement landscape opposite it. It lacked the domineering presence of the Royal Barracks, where anything up to 1,500 soldiers could be garrisoned at any one time in what became the oldest inhabited barracks in Europe. Instead, Ship Street came to house a small but important garrison connected to the castle. It remains today as office space, as well as providing a fine passageway through to the grounds of Dublin Castle and the Chester Beatty Library.

Ship Street Barracks Gate (Luke Fallon)

Ship Street Barracks is now best remembered for its role in the aftermath of the Easter Rising, housing primarily – but not exclusively – female prisoners. Helena Molony, Abbey actor and a member of the Irish Citizen Army garrison which had seized City Hall, remembered that:

> We were kept for eight days in the dirty room in Ship Street Barracks. It was a disused room at the back of the building, on the west side. There were old bits of mattresses in it, used by the soldiers. They were covered with vermin; and before a day had passed we were all covered with vermin too.[30]

In the subsequent revolutionary period, Ship Street Barracks was identified as a weak link in the imperial chain by the republican movement. Edward Handley, a World War One veteran who had been wounded in France, operated secretly within the British Army in procuring arms for the Irish Citizen Army, to which he was politically sympathetic. Of Ship Street, he recalled that, 'I was able to get a number of these rifles. I even got about five or six belonging to the Black and Tans stationed there. The Black and Tans were very often drunk so it was easy to take a rifle now and again.'[31] Ship Street Barracks was also utilised for court-martialling during the revolutionary years. On the same day in September 1919, a member of Dáil Éireann, Patrick O'Keefe TD, was tried for a speech 'calculated to cause sedition', while Liberty Hall's caretaker was tried for being in 'possession of a service rifle, an automatic pistol and some cartridges'.[32] More curious were the cases of two Australian soldiers, charged with 'marching at the head of a Sinn Féin procession … and with wearing Sinn Féin colours'.[33] It was a story that sadly the contemporary press did not elaborate on.

The conditions in which the people of Little Italy lived are difficult to picture today, with one side of Ship Street now largely replaced by modern hotel development. Some sense of the poverty can be gleaned, however, from a report on 'The Causes of Enteric Fever in the Dublin Garrison', penned by a British Military physician in 1890. While the barracks itself was a comparatively healthy physical space:

> I am sorry to say that the general sanitary condition of the vicinity – outside barracks – is the worst that could possibly be imagined. The approaches are by narrow streets … I had medical charge of these barracks during the summer, and I passed through these streets in discharge of my duties at various hours by day and night. Anything to come up to the offensive nature of the putrid emanations of these streets I never experienced before.[34]

Conditions on Ship Street were described as cramped, and the author was horrified by the presence of a dairy

177

amidst the tenements. What was required was a total reconfiguration of the district: 'The street must be widened, otherwise the barracks will never be healthy.'[35]

The soldiers, of course, are gone. The handing over of Dublin Castle in January 1922 took place with minimal fanfare, historian John Gibney describing it as 'an event devoid of ceremony, far removed from the familiar but completely fictional version in Neil Jordan's *Michael Collins*'.[36] There was no raising and lowering of flags, no quips on waiting 700 years, and not yet a Free State army to parade into the Castle grounds. Ship Street Barracks simply fell quiet a few months later, as the old order left.

The Italians lasted a little longer, before the new suburbanisation of the Free State spread them – like many inner-city communities – into the new hinterlands. On Chancery Lane, near Ship Street, a plaque of a hurdy-gurdy instrument with the words 'Little Italy' upon it, the work of artist Chris Reid, is the only clue of their presence here before.[37] In another way, Giuseppe Cervi is commemorated every time someone orders a 'One and One'.

9

Church Street

St Michan's Church, Church Street (Courtesy of Dublin City Library and Archive)

Walking along Church Street, beginning at the Father Mathew Bridge on the Liffey and heading for Constitution Hill, we pass places of great sadness in the story of the city and its working class, including the site of a tenement collapse in 1913. That disaster, at least, was a catalyst for change and brought about a damning housing inquiry the following year. A memorial marks the spot at which seven people were killed, while behind it we see the new housing that followed. A walk up Church Street also brings us past the site of Dublin's worst industrial accident, a horrific boiler explosion in 1878 which claimed fourteen lives and which is curiously forgotten.

The street has a broader story to tell, of course, and one which stretches back to the earliest days of Dublin. Long before Dublin 7 as we know it, Church Street was part of Oxmantown, the development that grew on the other side of the Liffey from the medieval walled town. More than being merely a part of it, it was its main thoroughfare. Dublin's foremost historian, David Dickson, tells us, 'by the end of the thirteenth century, the northside's particular association with markets, slaughterhouses and ironworking was already evident, by which time it equalled the walled town in area, if not in population.'[1] Oxmantown, like so many place names across the city, is a corruption of something else. Look instead to Ostman, a reference to the Vikings – *Eastmen*.[2] Some of the things which are still synonymous with this area and

its immediate surroundings, like the various market buildings, are part of a tradition of market commerce stretching
back centuries.

When we think of class division in Dublin throughout the centuries, traditionally the Liffey itself has been
thought of, rightly or wrongly, as a dividing line. This
has made its way into popular culture, most famously
in Roddy Doyle's *The Commitments*. 'In working class
Dublin semiotics,' Michael O'Sullivan wrote in his biography of Brendan Behan, 'the distinction between those
born on the Southside and those born on the Northside
was all-important.'[3]

Historically, there was a time when 'East-West' was
a better way of thinking of such things (and perhaps it
is once more). As a new, fashionable Dublin developed
to the east in the eighteenth century, real poverty was
to be found in the west, on both sides of the Liffey. The
Liberties had its equivalent across the river in the parish
of St Michan's. Church Street was at the heart of an area
which was long regarded as one of 'Dublin's poorest and
most densely-populated parishes'.[4]

These working class districts to the west may have
had economic hardship in common, but they were cul-
turally distinct, something they felt strongly enough about
to engage in occasional faction fighting, perhaps as much
sectarian as recreational. The primarily Protestant weavers of the southside Liberties, clashing with the largely
Catholic northside butchers and market workers known

as the Ormond Boys, was a feature of life in the eighteenth-century city, with the latter condemned as 'a set of
lawless desperadoes'.[5] They await *Peaky Blinders* or *Gangs
of New York*-style treatment.

Things remained difficult into the nineteenth century.
One guide to the city, published in 1835, warned that the
residents of this district were 'all of the poorest classes of
society; and so proverbial is this parish for its poverty, that
the advertisement of the annual charity sermon is headed
by the words "the poorest parish in Dublin"'.[6] Thomas
Willis, a Dublin apothecary who carried out an important
survey of the city a decade later, felt compelled to write
that, 'the worst districts are the Liberties on the south,
and the parish of St Michan on the northside of the city.'[7]
Municipal employee Nugent Robinson, speaking to the
Social Science Association in Dublin in 1861, referred
specifically to the parish of St Michan's as being among
the very worst districts in the city, insisting much of it was
'only fit to be demolished'. To him, 'the people inhabiting
these localities look as though stricken by the plague.'[8]

Walking up Church Street nowadays, we quickly
encounter the never-ending construction site that is
Hammond Lane, site of what has been described as
'one of Dublin's most notorious and long-standing
vacant plots of land'.[9] Earmarked for a new courts
building over many years and successive governments,
not much has happened on Hammond Lane in the
contemporary city.

Hammond Lane (Luke Fallon)

It's difficult to picture the Hammond Lane of the Victorian age, a busy place running off Church Street, with the foundry and ironworks of Messrs. Strong a significant local employer to men from throughout the district.

At around 1.30 p.m. on 27 April 1878, an explosion in the area of Hammond Lane caused panic and confusion. The *Freeman's Journal* noted that rumours abounded in the city, as:

> ... a terrific explosion was heard in the neighbourhood of Arran Quay and Church Street and in the Four Courts. Reports spread rapidly, and were, it is needless to say, of a very varied character.

One was that the Bow Street Distillery had been blown up; another that four houses had fallen. Those in the vicinity of Hammond Lane knew too well what had happened.[10]

At Strong's foundry, the steam boiler had exploded, bursting with a force that led *The Irish Times* to describe how 'one of the front walls of the foundry was rent into pieces, and literally blown into the street'.[11] A part of the boiler was described as having been 'violently hurled into a gateway opposite. Had it struck one of the houses filled with alarmed men, women and children, a terrible addition might have been made to the dreadful calamity.'[12]

The fear of such boiler explosions at the time was very real. Publications like *The Engineer*, first launched in the 1850s, repeatedly wrote of the risks of such incidents occurring, and in Britain lives were lost in such industrial accidents. Fifteen lives were lost at the Town and Son Factory at Bingley in West Yorkshire in June 1869 owing to a boiler explosion there, while an earlier explosion at Fieldhouse Mills in Rochdale claimed ten lives in 1855. In New York, the dreadful Hague Street explosion in 1850 had claimed more than sixty lives. In Dublin, the *Freeman's Journal* was furious that 'of late years, boiler explosion has followed boiler explosion with alarming and increasing frequency'.[13]

The loss of life on Hammond Lane could have been worse, as many men had left Strong's at one o'clock on their break. One premises destroyed by the powerful blast was Duffy's public house, opposite the foundry, where the proprietor, Patrick Duffy, and two of his children were killed. Mr Duffy was a well-known figure in Dublin, having held the position of warder in one of the Metropolitan convict depots, and having been employed by Dublin Corporation in the past. His public house would come to be described as 'a shambles, having collapsed like a pack of cards, burying those inside'.[14] Two of the tenement buildings on the street were destroyed too, three-storey buildings which housed some of the poorest workers in Dublin. Fourteen lives were ultimately lost, in an industrial tragedy on a scale previously unimaginable here.

Yet if there was hope for answers, people were to be left disappointed. Geraghty and Whitehead, in their history of the Dublin Fire Brigade, note that:

> The engineers' report stated that the boiler was not properly maintained and was weakened by corrosion. No independent engineer had examined the boiler in the previous two years … There were no statutory regulations under the Factories Act 1875 for the inspection of boilers, although such provision had been demanded from parliament by engineers throughout the United Kingdom.[15]

In the end, nobody was found negligent, and the tragedy quickly disappeared from the pages of Dublin newspapers, leaving the people of Hammond Lane to put the pieces back together again. It would not be the last tragedy to befall the people of the Church Street area, nor the final report into scandalous events here.

Despite the changing times, one thing that has remained on Church Street through much turbulence is St Michan's Church, which for some six centuries was the only parish church north of the Liffey.[16] In some form or another, a church has stood at this site since 1095, though it is the 1686 church of architect William Robinson, with plenty of later additions, we largely see now.

An unusual postcard showing 'mummies in the vaults, St. Michan's Church, Dublin.' (Courtesy of Dublin City Library and Archive)

Few visitors come to see Robinson's architecture. St Michan's instead has become something of a Dark Tourism attraction, drawing those who wish to enter its vaults and see the mummified remains on display there. Journeying down its narrow stone stairway, it remains one of the most curious visitor experiences in the city. It has been drawing people – the generally morbid and the generally curious – for centuries. Some ponder if Bram Stoker, author of *Dracula,* was influenced by the vaults, though there is no strong evidence that he visited. Stoker's imagination owed more to the cholera epidemic of 1832 that ravaged Sligo, something his mother would write of in detail and which transfixed him. The folk and supernatural tales learned in the parlour of 1 Merrion Square, home of Sir William Wilde and Lady Jane Wilde, shaped his mind too.

Bram may not have ventured down the stone stairs of St Michan's, but plenty of other writers did in his lifetime, including the travel writers of their day. In *Picturesque Ireland*, published in 1890, readers were told how these bodies came to be:

> The floor, walls and atmosphere of the vaults of St. Michan's are perfectly dry, the flooring is even covered with dust, and the walls are composed of a stone peculiarly calculated to resist moisture. This combination of circumstances contributes to aid nature in rendering the atmosphere of those gloomy regions more dry than the atmosphere we enjoy.[17]

187

A visitor to St Michan's, *Picturesque Ireland* tells us, will learn that, 'bodies deposited there have been kept for centuries in such a state of preservation as to keep the features discernible, and the bones, cartilages and skin astonishingly perfect.'[18]

The lives of those in the vaults of St Michan's, like 'The Crusader' of some eight centuries past, are intriguing things to ponder. Others in the vaults are better and clearer understood, like John and Henry Sheares, two revolutionary brothers of the 1798 insurrection who went to their deaths on the gallows at nearby Newgate Prison holding hands. They had witnessed what was once totally unimaginable: a monarch going to the guillotine. On his return from France, John Sheares was seen 'to exhibit with delight a handkerchief stained with the royal blood of the unhappy king'.[19] Beside them is the death mask of Theobald Wolfe Tone.

And Robert Emmet? Some maintained that the body of Emmet, publicly executed in September 1803 before a giddy, jostling crowd in the Liberties, was ultimately laid to rest in the grounds of St Michan's. Emmet famously insisted in the court which found him guilty that no epitaph to him should be penned in an unfree Ireland. There are numerous versions of Emmet's speech from the dock, typical of the time and the power of press and politics, but in one he proclaimed:

> Yes, my Lords, a man who does not wish to have his
> epitaph written until his country is liberated will not

The grave of Robert Emmet? Elinor Wiltshire Collection
(National Library of Ireland)

leave a weapon in the power of envy, nor a pretence
to impeach the probity which he means to preserve
even in the grave to which tyranny consigns him.

The historian R. R. Madden, a faithful chronicler of
the story of the United Irishmen, published his biography of Emmet in 1847, mere decades after the Emmet
insurrection had failed. He spoke to some elderly

Dubliners, who informed him of various places Emmet was said to be buried. Madden went to visit the theorised spot in St. Michan's churchyard, and pondered, 'is this the tomb that was not to be inscribed, till other times, and other men, could do justice to the memory of the person whose grave had been the subject of my inquiries?'[20]

Where Emmet rests, alas, remains something of a mystery. As for the epitaph? Peadar O'Donnell, a veteran of the Anti-Treaty IRA of the Civil War who would remain a political radical into the heated political milieu of the 1930s, would conclude one pamphlet with the words:

> That is why such phrases as 'when we won our independence' is resented by so many people – it is dangerously near the ultimate blasphemy – 'Emmet's Epitaph may now be written'.[21]

Emmet Fever in 1903, against the backdrop of the centenary of his passing, led to a renewed wave of interest in the question of where the young patriot lay buried. At that time, there was digging at St Peter's Church at Aungier Street, another rumoured resting place. One of those at the scene was Dr Thomas Addis Emmet, great-nephew to Robert Emmet. Nothing was uncovered. Even today, questions remain as to where Emmet rests.

There is no mystery surrounding the events of 2 September 1913, when Church Street witnessed the tragic collapse of two tenement homes, numbers 66 and 67. Facing the beautiful St Mary of the Angels Church, the church of the Capuchin Order, these houses were typical of the tenement buildings that were to be found in Dublin's inner-city. The 1911 Census had revealed that some sixty-three per cent of the population of the city were working class, with about forty-five per cent of these in tenement accommodation. It was estimated that some 37,500 Dubliners were 'housed in dwellings so decayed as to be on the borderline of unfitness for human habitation'.[22]

By the time of the Church Street tenement collapses, there was growing agitation within local politics on the question of Dublin's housing crisis. In 1911, Dublin Corporation passed a motion which acknowledged:

> That the question of the abolition of the slums in which a very large portion of Dublin's working class population are housed, and the substitution therefore of decent dwellings at moderate rent has become so pressing that it is imperative that some decisive steps should be taken to deal with it immediately.[23]

While a housing committee was established, it was slow to move into action, not meeting until 1913.

What occurred at Church Street was not without precedent in the city, where dangerous tenement

Commemorative plaque to the victims of the Church Street tenement collapse (Luke Fallon)

blocks did give way on occasion. Joseph O'Brien, in his important and still often drawn upon study, *Dear, Dirty Dublin: A City in Distress, 1899–1916*, gives one particularly interesting example that tells us much: 'In 1902 the collapse of a tenement in Townsend Street killed one person and injured others. What was embarrassing about this case was that the building was owned by Alderman O'Reilly of Trinity Ward, a member of the Health Committee.'[24] In April 1911, several condemned houses near the intersection of North King Street and Church Street collapsed, though their tenants had already been evicted.

As far back as July 1911, there were questions around the stability of 66 and 67 Church Street, though the inspecting officer judged 67 safe after recommended minor repairs were carried out.

It was about 8.45 p.m. when tragedy struck. Chris Corlett, author of a history of the tragedy, notes that, 'it appears that the chimney gave way, crashing through the house as it fell and pushing the front wall out into the street.' These inter-connected, subdivided homes of the poor collapsed like a pack of cards, claiming the lives of Hugh Sammon (17), Elizabeth Sammon (4½), Nicholas Fitzpatrick (40), Elizabeth Fagan (50), John Shiels (3), Peter Crowley (6) and Margaret Rourke (55).[25]

The collapse of tenement homes in Dublin was shocking to the inhabitants of the city, of course, but Church Street's tragedy reverberated much further away.

In the international press, Dublin was the centre of much coverage, as a city engulfed in unprecedented labour strife. Not alone did these houses collapse during the Lockout, when tens of thousands of Dublin labourers were ordered to leave the Irish Transport and General Workers' Union (ITGWU) or lose employment, it emerged that one of the victims, Hugh Sammon, had been locked out of work the previous day.

Church Street propelled questions around housing, and the living conditions of the poor of the city, to the top of the agenda. Jim Larkin, the firebrand leader of the ITGWU, would compare the conditions of the Dublin working class unfavourably to those of prisoners:

> In Mountjoy Gaol – where I have had the honour to reside on more than one occasion – criminals were allowed 400 cubic feet. Yet men who slave and work, and their women – those beautiful women we have among the working classes – are compelled to live, many of them, five in a room, with less than 300 cubic feet. They are taken from their mother's breasts at an early age, and are used up as material is used up in a fire. These are some of the conditions that obtain in this Catholic city of Dublin, the most church-going city, I believe, in the world.[26]

Larkin, his faithful follower James Plunkett remembered, was 'no doctrinaire revolutionary in the continental sense and he was no great theorist'. To Plunkett, 'his lifelong concern was not with theory, but with the immediate needs of the underprivileged man – the sweated man, the struggling mothers, the little children born to a life of drudge in a sunless world.' Plunkett could acknowledge the difficulties of Larkin, and how 'he was sometimes arrogant, sometimes unfair to colleagues and often rash beyond the justification of his most indulgent admirers'.[27] In the politics of Larkinism, which sought to shine a light on the realities of people's lives and convince them of the possibilities of something better, events like Church Street were damning verdicts against the existing order.

Sammon, readers of the Larkinite newspaper *The Irish Worker* were told, would be remembered as a hero, while those who had attempted to smash the union would be viewed with contempt by history. The tragedy of Church Street did focus public attention, at last, on the issue of housing in the city in a new way that could no longer be ignored.

The findings of the subsequent inquiry were damning with regards members of Dublin Corporation's elected council, revealing that, 'no fewer than sixteen members of the council (only one of them a Unionist) owned between then eighty-nine tenements and second-class houses.'[28]

There were other councillors for whom this issue was close to home and now firmly beyond talking points. Labour and trade union-aligned representatives seized upon the public feeling, but so too did Alderman Thomas Kelly of Sinn Féin, who came from a working-class tenement background.

The Easter Rising, in many ways, made Sinn Féin (though the press and politicians wrongly convinced themselves that the very opposite was true). Sinn Féin before 1916 is not thought of as a significant political force, one historian writing of how, 'while Home Rule still had a hope of passage … Sinn Féin remained politically obscure, seeing little success until 1918, when it represented the sole political alternative to the Redmondites.'[29] This was perhaps true nationally, but there was one great exception, which was Dublin Corporation. Here, the party was represented by very capable voices that would include W. T. Cosgrave, later first President of the Executive of the Irish Free State.

The presence of the townships, which had taken much of the Unionist political voice into the new hinterlands, ensured the Corporation offered a battleground in which Sinn Féin could compete. What Sinn Féin stood for in the early twentieth century was sometimes unclear, even contradictory, reflecting the broad nature of something still lacking cohesion. On housing, and matters of municipal corruption, however, Kelly was to prove a lightning rod. His response to the 1914 housing inquiry is still a powerful read, more than a century on:

I assert that the main cause of the social evils of Dublin is the dire poverty of the major portion of the working classes, which is the greatest barrier to social progress. It is all very well for those who have never lived in them to hold up their hands in horror of those tall, haunt, repulsive tenement houses; but those who, like myself, lived in them for years, know that life amongst the poor is only made tolerable by the help which one poor family renders another in times of stress.[30]

Kelly's name is associated with great progress in housing in the years that followed the Church Street tragedy, his biographer maintaining that his 'most enduring legacy from his

Church Street Housing Scheme (Courtesy of Dublin City Library and Archive)

197

long public service career is the influence he had on the development of local authority housing in Dublin'.[31] The beautiful houses which came to occupy Church Street and the surrounding area, visible in the Housing Committee map of just four years later, are a testament to his commitment to seeking change. We see Kelly's name on the map as chairman, along with the name of Dublin's City Architect, C. J. McCarthy, who made these homes a reality.

Kelly's influence is to be found on the other side of the Liffey too, with the early 1920s Fairbrothers' Fields scheme, now widely known as The Tenters, in Dublin 8. Very little happened in Dublin housing between the Church Street housing scheme and The Tenters, reflecting war-time inflation and political instability.

★★★

Much has changed on Church Street since the 1913 tragedy, but one welcome constant has been the presence of the Capuchin Order, on the street since 1690 (not recalled as a particularly good year by Irish Catholics, bringing with it the Protestant King William III's victory at the Boyne). Stepping inside J. J. McCarthy's church, the altar is the work of James Pearse, while there are statues by sculptor Leo Broe in the entrance facade.

The Capuchin influence over the area was, and remains, strong. Today, Brother Kevin Crowley and his team in the Capuchin Day Centre serve hundreds of meals daily to those in need, a service they have been providing since the 1960s. When interviewed about this work in the press, Brother Kevin told a reporter proudly, 'I'm the CEO of the Capuchin Day Centre and my salary is nil.'[32] In 2018, Pope Francis visited the Capuchin Day Centre, meeting not only Brother Kevin but those who depend on him and his team.

Capuchin influence in the area once included the nearby Father Mathew Hall, built in honour of the 'Apostle of Temperance'. Formally opened in 1891, the building was an important social hub for the area which included a drama group, a cycling club, and a wide range of social and cultural activities designed to further the Temperance agenda. Father Theobald Mathew's nineteenth-century crusade against alcohol, and his conviction that 'Ireland sober is Ireland free', had far-reaching impacts in Irish society. The visiting Frederick Douglass, in Ireland in 1845, was among those to take 'the pledge', believing in Father Mathew's cause and that, 'all great reforms go together.'[33] In doing so, Douglass joined the millions of others who had taken 'the pledge', from Ireland and its diaspora.

A statue of Father Mathew looks down on Church Street from the building, but in time the building became more synonymous with the cause of cultural nationalism than Temperance. Not alone did it host meetings of the

Gaelic League in the years before insurrection, it served as a field kitchen (and then field hospital) during the Easter Rising, when the area around Church Street witnessed some of the fiercest fighting. A local child, 2-year-old Seán Foster from nearby Olaf Road in Stoneybatter, was shot in his pram in the opening moments of the rebellion. His mother had encountered her own brother on a Church Street rebel barricade. As she rushed towards Father Mathew Hall after shooting opened up on the street, her brother heard her cry in anguish, 'they've killed my baby!'[34] On nearby North King Street, a brutal massacre of civilians in their homes by members of the South Staffordshire Regiment further contributed to the horrors of Easter Week for local residents. A story told by one Volunteer in recollections to the Bureau of Military History gives a sense of just how dangerous Church Street and its immediate environs were during the fighting:

> At one stage while we were in the Father Mathew Hall feelings were getting rather tense. It was alleged by somebody that some members of the unit were not taking their fair share of the risks at the barricades, that they preferred to remain with the Cumann na mBan in the kitchen rather than go out and risk their necks. A young Volunteer by the name of Howard left the Hall to take up a position at one of the barricades. A short time later he was killed there.[35]

A reminder that cities are ever-changing is found at the intersection of Church Street and Stirrup Lane, where a mural entitled 'Horse Boy' by the street art group Subset honours a piece of nearby local heritage, the Smithfield Horse Fair. Subset's work across the city has come and gone, reflecting its sometimes ambiguous legal status.

A market traditionally held on the first Sunday of March and September, the Smithfield Horse Fair long attracted not merely buyers and sellers of horses but observers of the human condition. Wally Cassidy's photographic collection, *Smithfield Horse Fair Dublin 1990–93*, is particularly good, but photographers have long been drawn to see the last vestiges of what was once a thriving tradition of inner-city horse fairs. Smithfield, as Bill Barich had it in his great account of the changing Irish public house, 'belongs to the new city of glass and steel, not the old one of bricks and mortar, but it regains a bit of soul when the horse fair, a centuries-old tradition, occurs.'[36] Subset's piece has led to some confrontation with the authorities, entangled in a years-long planning dispute. It brings great colour and vibrancy, like other Subset works across the city.

A collective shrouded in secrecy, one member of the group said in a recent interview that, 'the one thing we all sort of seem to agree on is that Dublin and Ireland need more artwork and more colour.'[37]

10

Eustace Street

A view up Eustace Street (Courtesy of Dublin City Library and Archive)

Having recently suffered the abasement of being ranked amongst the world's ten most disappointing tourist destinations by the *Huffington Post* (to whom it seemed little more than 'a prime example of the rampant fleecing of drunken tourists'), Temple Bar is an area which has long struggled with an identity crisis.[1]

The streetscape of Eustace Street remains predominantly eighteenth century and succeeds in maintaining some of the historic character of the Temple Bar district, a broader district that was arguably more transformed by the 1970s than the 1790s.

The street takes its name from Sir Maurice Eustace, a former Lord Chancellor of Ireland who resided there following his appointment in the mid-seventeenth century. His house – or, more specifically, townhouse – was showy, described as 'particularly elaborate', and signified his social status.[2] No trace of Damask, the name he bestowed on the residence, remains.

Eustace Street, perhaps more than any other street in the capital, is a street of ideas. Its story is entangled not only with the development of republican separatism in the 1790s, but with the cause of the abolition of slavery and with the development of Ireland's small but influential Quaker community.

Once, Temple Bar's importance lay in its proximity to the former Custom House, constructed in 1707, and sitting just to the east of what we now know as Grattan Bridge. Its construction 'served to harmonise

commercial, financial and residential developments
about that pontine point'.[3] Named in honour of Sir
William Temple, provost of Trinity College from 1609 to
1627, the area was a warren of busy streets of production
and industry in the eighteenth and nineteenth-century
city. That working life and industrial past is still visible in
the presence of a former workers' guild hall, Merchant's
Arch, which leads us through into the district from the
Ha'penny Bridge. The hustle and bustle of production
has been replaced by a thriving tourist economy – in
normal times, at least. The eeriness of the cobbled streets
of Temple Bar during the Covid-19 pandemic revealed
the disconnect between the district and the broader city,
as well as recalling the words of former Dublin City
Council planner Paul Kearns: 'Dublin has, for far too
long, favoured the temporary, often fleeting visitor, over
the local urban resident.'[4]

The arrival of a new Custom House in 1791, which
radically shifted the entire axis of the city, was the beginning of a period of mixed fortunes for Temple Bar that
continued well into the second half of the twentieth
century. What was envisioned in the 1970s for Temple
Bar was not so much urban renewal as urban deletion,
with a proposed transportation hub for Córas Iompair
Éireann (CIÉ), which would have swallowed up the old
and replaced it with a central bus station for the capital.
In acquiring property with the eventual aim of demolition, the bus company began leasing out units at low

rents. Paul Knox, in a study on radical transformation in urban districts internationally, makes the point that this had an unexpected effect:

> Paradoxically, this triggered a process of revitalization. Activities which could afford only low rents on short leases moved into the district. These included artists' studios, galleries, recording and rehearsal studies, pubs and cafes, second-hand clothes shops, small boutiques, bookshops and record stores, as well as a number of voluntary organisations. Together with the district's architectural character, the youth culture attracted by the district's new commercial tenants brought a neo-bohemian atmosphere to Temple Bar.[5]

Some of that excitement has been lost. Gone is the Hirschfeld Centre and Flikkers Disco, the birthplace of electronic music in the capital. Gone too is the Eager Beaver and the Dublin Resource Centre on Crow Street. Temple Bar today may not bring 'neo-bohemian' to mind, but a surprising array of institutions from that moment of great optimism remain in the district, including the Temple Bar Gallery and Studios and the Project Arts Theatre. There is also the brilliant Meeting House Square, accessible from a number of entrances, including one off Eustace Street, and which hosts all from food markets to film screenings.

The district's association with revelry, and in particular with the industry of stag and hen parties, is more familiar internationally. In 1998, the *Irish Independent* reported how 'stag parties have given Dublin tourism chiefs such a multi-million pound headache they have banned them in Temple Bar'.[6] Such a ludicrous ban was, at its core, unenforceable. The leprechaun hats lived to fight another day.

There is a certain irony at play; an area many consider to be overrun with public houses today has essentially always been thus, albeit with very different public houses. Indeed, in the days of the United Irishmen, more pubs occupied these streets. One such historic pub is marked by a plaque today on Eustace Street: The Eagle Tavern. And one leading United Irishman who had a link to the pub was James Napper Tandy.

Napper Tandy was a long-established radical voice in the city before the establishment of the Society of United Irishmen, even once proclaiming himself as 'the leader of the malcontents'.[7] The son of an iron monger and a successful wine merchant in the city, he served on the common council of Dublin Corporation and came to be a respected figure to the proletariat of the Irish capital, who saw in him a representative of their own ambitions.

In times of discontent, they looked to Napper Tandy for guidance. When construction began on the new Custom House in 1781, a full decade before completion, it infuriated many who felt it would negatively impact on their own livelihoods. Under his direction, they marched onto the site and levelled the fencing, making their displeasure clear. Some labelled Tandy the real lord mayor of the city. Whatever he declared himself to be, the view of leading historian of eighteenth-century radicalism Jim Smyth is clear: Tandy's 'influence over Dublin's lower classes was immense,' and he was 'a real force in the municipal and street politics of the capital'.[8]

Politics, of course, happens not only in the chambers of parliament. Much change occurs on the streets. The events which shook French society in 1789 encouraged some to take to the streets of Dublin and Belfast, as they did each Bastille Day in the years that followed. The French Revolution, the *Freeman's Journal* mocked, 'may give the shop boy a pleasing opportunity of appearing in the disguise of a military officer, or enable the merchant's clerk to personate a hero.' Reflecting on the French Revolution, and the public conflict of pamphlets, letters and ideas which came from it, Theobald Wolfe Tone remembered it as a time of awakening:

> Mr. Burke's famous invective appeared; and this in due season produced Paine's reply, which he called *Rights of Man*. This controversy, and the gigantic event which gave rise to it, changed in an instant the politics of Ireland. Two years before, the nation was in lethargy.[9]

On 9 November 1791, less than two years after the fall of the Bastille, men gathered in The Eagle Tavern to establish a Dublin branch of the Society of United Irishmen. In the chair was none other than James Napper Tandy.

The society began life as a body committed not to revolution but reform. Just eighteen men attended that first gathering, at which they passed a resolution which welcomed 'the present great era of reform, when unjust governments are falling in every quarter of Europe', and which pledged the Society to seek reform and 'equal representation of all the people in parliament'.[10] A circular issued weeks later, and carrying the signature of Napper Tandy, spoke of 'common rights' and 'common wrongs':

> The object of this institution is to make a United Society of the Irish Nation: To make all Irishmen Citizens – all Citizens Irishmen – nothing appearing to us more natural at all times, and at this crisis in Europe more seasonable, than that those who have common interests and common enemies, who suffer common wrongs, and lay claims to common rights, should know each other, and should act together. In our opinion, ignorance has been the demon of discord, which has so long deprived Irishmen not only of the blessings of well-regulated government, but even the common benefits of civil society.[11]

The society would be criminalised and driven underground in 1793, and meetings like that at The Eagle Tavern were replaced with clandestine gatherings. Within seven short years, there was insurrection, in what Irish popular memory has recalled as 'The Year of the French', 1798. To some, Dublin would become 'the dog that didn't bark', the insurrection largely playing out in the west and south of the country.[12] But it had been the two primary urban centres of Ireland, Belfast and Dublin, where the ideas of the conspiracy fermented.

In trying to imagine the atmosphere around the table in taverns like The Eagle in that moment of transformation, recalled to human history as the Age of Revolution, we gather some semblance of what it was like from the surviving accounts of political toasts raised at United Irish gatherings. As Martyn Powell has noted, 'the toast had a complex impact upon those present, creating an additional degree of unity and resolve, a collective bonhomie, and an awareness of a shared past and a common set of goals in the present.'[13] Toasts were raised to the health of men like radical philosopher Thomas Paine and George Washington, the guiding lights of the American Revolution, but some were more imaginative: 'Confusion to the enemies of French liberty!' was popular, as was 'the spirit of the French mob to the people of Ireland!'[14]

★★★

The Eagle Tavern has been lost to time, and so we can no longer step inside of the room where the United

Irish conspiracy began in Dublin. Still, just a few doors away, we can sit in the very space where the abolitionist Frederick Douglass spoke in 1845 during his speaking tour of the island of Ireland.

The United Irishmen were resolutely opposed to slavery, even hosting the celebrated abolitionist and former slave Olaudah Equiano on a speaking tour of the island in 1791. The island left a deep impression on Equiano, who recalled: 'I was everywhere exceedingly well treated by persons of all ranks.'[15] A Dublin edition of his memoir, *The Interesting Narrative of the Life of Olaudah Equiano*, was published with the support of prominent United Irishmen who subscribed towards it, including Napper Tandy. When Douglass arrived in Ireland some five decades later, his hosts on Eustace Street were not the United Irishmen – by then a memory – but the Society of Friends, better known as the Quakers.

The Quakers, non-conformist Christians, had their origins in the preaching of George Fox, the son of a Leicestershire weaver born in 1624. In the eyes of some, the Quakers were blasphemers, while to others they were viewed as subversive of social and political order. With no clergy, liturgy or sacraments, Quakers preached publicly of the 'Inner Light' they felt was the path to God. David Booy, editor of a collection of Quaker memoirs, tells us that, 'in the early years of the movement, Friends were notorious for going to churches and speaking out after the sermon to rebut what the minister had said and proclaim their own beliefs.' Meeting Houses like that on Eustace Street emerged, 'where they simply waited on God in silence until led to speak. The intensity of their spiritual experience made them tremble or quake: hence their name, first applied in derision.'[16] Quakers maintained a social radicalism, believing in the need to proactively campaign for societal change. Born in September 1839, the Hibernian Anti-Slavery Society reflected this commitment; six of its nine committee members were Quakers.[17]

Three Dublin Quakers of that era, James Haughton, Richard Allen and Richard D. Webb, were all dedicated social reformers, active on a wide range of issues that spanned everything from temperance to opposing capital punishment. Dublin wits labelled them 'the Anti-Everythingarians', while Haughton's vegetarianism led a political rival to mockingly brand him 'the Vegetable Haughton'. Such insults did not faze them; the trio were amongst those to attend an international anti-slavery conference in London in 1840. Daniel O'Connell, who spoke before that same gathering, had an electric effect on the attendees, leading abolitionist William Lloyd Garrison to remark that O'Connell's speeches on slavery had the power to 'scathe like lightning, and smite like thunderbolts. No man, in the wide world, has spoken so strongly against the soul-drivers of this land as O'Connell'.[18]

In 1845, Webb was the central figure in arranging the Irish speaking arrangements for Frederick Douglass,

211

the escaped slave from Maryland whose text *Narrative of the Life of Frederick Douglass, an American Slave* was a moving and infuriating account of struggle. Standing at the plaque currently honouring Douglass on Eustace Street, a keen eye will note it differs from other plaques to historical figures in Dublin in not listing a year of birth. The reason for this is explained in the very first words we read in his text:

> I was born in Tuckahoe, near Hillsborough, and about twelve miles from Easton, in Talbot County, Maryland. I have no accurate knowledge of my age, never having seen any authentic record containing it. By far the larger part of the slaves know as little of their ages as horses know of theirs, and it is the wish of most masters within my knowledge to keep their slaves thus ignorant. I do not remember to have ever met a slave who could tell of his birthday. They seldom come nearer to it than planting-time, harvest-time, cherry-time, spring-time, or fall-time. A want of information concerning my own was a source of unhappiness to me even during childhood.[19]

Douglass would spend months in Ireland, his speaking appearances attracting much media attention. When he spoke at the Friends Meeting House on 9 September, the press noted that, 'his frame is robust, he is above the

Frederick Douglass (Library of Congress)

middle size, and has a very pleasing expression of coun-
tenance.'[20] Americans, Douglass told the packed hall, 'are
very sensitive to the opinion of the world'. He implored
the audience to keep up this opinion, by making 'every
American slave holder, every American apologist of slavery, who set his feet upon our soil feel that he was in

213

a land of freedom, among a people that hated oppression, and who loved liberty – liberty for all, for the black man as well as the white man – to make them feel they breathed in a pure anti-slavery atmosphere.'[21] Days later, on 12 September, Douglass spoke in the Quakers hall once more, moving one journalist enough to proclaim that, 'he is a striking evidence that God has not placed the black man in a grade below the whites in the scale of creation, and that it is monstrous for the latter to hold the former in bondage on any such pretence.'[22]

Webb's work ensured the printing of a Dublin 1845 edition of the *Narrative*, with an initial print run of 2,000 copies quickly bought up across the island of Ireland. Douglass earned $750 from the initial Dublin edition of the work, and also directly influenced its content, from introduction to illustration. In Ireland, Patricia J. Ferreira has noted, 'he was free to behave and speak as he desired, Douglass's capacity to manage his own affairs flourished.'[23] Ireland left a deep impact on Douglass, writing home that, 'instead of the bright, blue sky of America, I am covered with the soft, grey fog of the Emerald Isle. I breathe, and lo! The chattel becomes a man.'[24]

★★★

The venue in which Douglass spoke is now a part of the Irish Film Institute, home on Eustace Street since 1992. Sitting in Screen 1, there are still reminders of the former life of the site, including fine window frames and a door, now leading to nowhere, that once opened onto a gallery. Leading architectural firm O'Donnell and Tuomey reimagined the Quaker Meeting House, or most of it, towards the goal of an arthouse cinema. Former IFI Director David Kavanagh has described how, 'the Quaker community asked for closed bids which had to describe the intended use of the building. We proposed the lowest price we thought feasible – which we did not have – and had to ask the Quakers to allow a delay in payment while we raised the money to make the purchase.'[25]

Arthouse cinemas in the city are recalled as a small part of the battle against censorship, given that their membership structure ensured the inability of the film censor to dictate their programming. The state's first film censor, James Montgomery, professed that he knew little about cinema but, 'took the Ten Commandments as his guide.'[26] Appointed in 1923 (the time of silent movies), Montgomery was amongst the first state-appointed censors in the field anywhere in the world. Describing his approach to cinema, his biographer tells us that, 'his strongest objections were to partial nudity, stage-Irishness, drunkenness, sensuality, anti-Catholicism, un-Christian ideas such as reincarnation, hula dancing, kissing, the portrayal of co-education in American films, bigamy, vulgarity, and violence.'[27]

Certainly, some Dublin cinemas emerged from a desire to circumvent Irish censorship. The Irish

Grace Plunkett (nee Gifford) cartoon showing censor James Montgomery bringing modesty to the *Venus de Milo* (National Library of Ireland)

Film Theatre, born in 1977 and housed on Earlsfort Terrace, operated on a membership basis that ensured

the film censor had no power over its programming,
as works were not being shown to the general public.
Some pondered the logic in all of this, viewing it as
an Irish solution to an Irish problem. The *Sunday Press*
noted how 'several thousand people could, for a price,
see films that did not go through the state-paid censor
in his office, a few hundred yards away,' while the Irish
Film Theatre received funding from the Arts Council.[28]
The IFT, which folded less than a decade after opening its doors, brought works by directors like Pier Paolo
Pasolini and Bernardo Bertolucci to Dublin, while also
giving Dubliners a chance to see the city on the big
screen in Joseph Strick's ambitious 1967 adaptation of
Ulysses. Ireland had never banned *Ulysses* in printed form,
but Milo O'Shea and Barbara Jefford's antics on screen
were considered too much for Irish eyes. Internationally,
the film was sometimes shown to segregated audiences –
in New Zealand, it was reportedly shown in some cities
in 'two cinemas, one for men and one for women'.[29] At
least they got to see it.

The Irish Film Institute emerged from a very different cinema tradition, and the National Film Institute,
which had been founded under the patronage of Dublin's
Catholic Archbishop, John Charles McQuaid, in 1943.
The NFI had ambitious plans 'to direct and encourage
the use of the motion picture in the national and cultural interests of the Irish people, in accordance with the
teachings of His Holiness, Pope Pius XI in the Encyclical,

Vigilanti Cura'.[30] Reflecting McQuaid's desire to influence Irish public taste, viewing committees were established in London and Hollywood 'to vet the suitability of films for import into Ireland'.[31] By the 1980s, church influence over the NFI had declined significantly, and in 1982 references to *Vigilanti Cura* were removed from the articles of association, and the body renamed.

Waning religious influence has not only bestowed Eustace Street with a world-class cinema, these days unconcerned with clerical guidance, but has also left it with a magnificent children's theatre. The Ark, at 11A Eustace Street, has taken up residence in what was formerly a Presbyterian Meeting House, constructed in the late 1720s. A striking red-brick with large sash windows and tall doors, the building still has the look of a sombre place of worship, but stepping inside it reveals the playful renovation of the 1990s that allowed it to become a creative space for children, one of the first of its kind internationally.

Abiding proof that history can hide in plain sight is found nearing the intersection of Eustace Street and East Essex Street, where St Winifred's Well is found, uncovered during renovations of the district in the early 1990s. Like St Brigid, St Winifred was long associated with wells and springs, though how a well in medieval Dublin came to bear her name remains something of a mystery, as Winifred lived in north Wales. It was pondered in the nineteenth century if its presence

9 Church Street

Houses of the Church Street development (Luke Fallon)

The art group Subset's 'Horse Boy' mural (Luke Fallon)

10 Eustace Street

James Napper Tandy, a prominent United Irishman and self-pro-
claimed 'leader of the malcontents' (National Gallery of Ireland)

Plaque to the United Irishmen (Luke Fallon)

11 Pearse Street

Carved heads of members of the Dublin Metropolitan Police at
Pearse Street Garda Station (Luke Fallon)

The Central Fire Station, designed by C. J. McCarthy
(Luke Fallon)

A poster for the Queen's Theatre (National Library of Ireland)

Commemorative plaque at the Science Gallery, Trinity College Dublin, honouring the firefighters who died during a blaze at Exide Batteries in October 1936 (Luke Fallon)

Pearse & Sons (Luke Fallon)

The Antient Concert Rooms building today (Luke Fallon)

Lady Gregory by John Butler Yeats
(National Gallery of Ireland)

Poster for an event in the Antient Concert Rooms featuring leading nationalists of the day (National Library of Ireland)

12 Moore Street

F. X. Buckley's mosaic tiling, a business promising meat 'Par Excellence' since the 1930s (Luke Fallon)

The Moore Street dragon (Luke Fallon)

A contemporary street stall on Moore Street (Luke Fallon)

St Winifred's Well (Courtesy of Dublin City Library and Archive)

'may indicate a Welsh place of worship in that locality, now probably superseded by the Scotch Church or the Quaker Meeting House'.[32]

The well, like the nearby Isolde's Tower on Exchange Street Lower (part of Dublin's historic walled defences, now preserved and on view through railings below an apartment block) reminds us of the rich archaeological work done in the Temple Bar area in the early 1990s, when the layers of history here revealed themselves. Archaeology, one commentator noted of 1990s Temple Bar, 'becomes an integral part of urban renewal.'[33]

That so many cultural institutions still call Temple Bar home is perhaps cause for Dubliners to reconsider their feelings on the district. Every metropolis has its points of contention. A protagonist in a novel set in New York City, reflecting on Times Square, tells us how, 'I usually do everything I can to avoid it. We all do. Hating Times Square is a New York point of pride. We're supposed to hate everything that tourists like.'[34] Similarly, even the most loving guide to Edinburgh complains of 'the tawdry tourist traps that now punctuate the Royal Mile'.[35]

The writer Anne Simpson, who penned *Blooming Dublin* in 1991 as a cross-examination of Irish society that revealed deep contradictions and contestations, told her readers:

> One of the pleasures of a recent visit was the sight of a rejuvenated Temple Bar, an artisans' neighbourhood ... With its sympathetic industrial conversions, its artistic colony – the Project Arts Centre and the Irish Film Institute are here – and the beginnings of an ethnic restaurant culture, this compact but irregular stretch possesses something of the variegated interest found in the Marais in Paris before it become ultra-modish, a quality which still exists in the shrunken workers' quarters of New York's Lower East Side.[36]

In 2021, a controversial proposed hotel development in the Merchant's Arch passageway caused real reflection on the district, but also reminded us that it still includes the Project Arts Centre, the New Theatre, the Irish Film Institute, the Gallery of Photography, the Ark Theatre, the Smock Alley Theatre and more among its inhabitants.[37] Some of what Simpson felt represented a positive turn for the city remains.

There may be not one Temple Bar, but several.

11

Pearse Street
(to Westland Row)

As Gaeilge, Pearse Street is listed as *Sráid an Phiarsaigh*, a name that honours Patrick Henry Pearse, otherwise known as Pádraig Mac Piarais.[1] School principal, writer and radical separatist, it was Pearse who read the proclamation of the Irish Republic at the General Post Office on O'Connell Street in the opening moments of the Easter Rising.

Nearby, Pearse Station is *Stáisiún na bPiarsach*, a name that encompasses commemoration of both Patrick and his younger brother, the artist and sculptor, William Pearse. It is undoubtedly the latter name that Patrick, tremendously close to and protective of young William, would prefer. There is something especially tragic in Patrick's final letter to his mother from a Kilmainham

WILLIAM PEARSE
(Executed in Kilmainham Prison, 4th May, 1916).

Commemorative postcard, Willie Pearse (Courtesy of Dublin City
Library and Archive)

Gaol cell outlining his sorrow at leaving her and his
brother behind, perhaps feeling that his own prominence

223

in the Rising and the proclamation had doomed him to execution, but that his less involved brother would survive. He had little idea that William would ultimately face the same end: a firing squad. Desmond Ryan, a 1916 Volunteer in the GPO and later a historian of the revolutionary period, recounted seeing William as the Rising intensified: "'A curious business", says Willie to me as he passes, "I wonder how it will end?",'[2]

Pearse Street is one of the longest streets in the capital, stretching from College Street all the way to Grand Canal Dock at Seán Mac Mahon Bridge. There is a walk of some fifteen minutes, at a relaxed pace, in exploring Pearse Street.

Once, this street carried the name Great Brunswick Street, taken from King George and the House of Brunswick-Lüneburg. Changing a street name is not merely a way of commemorating one person, but displacing another. In this sense, there are two political gestures in it.[3] That the birthplace of Pearse should be commemorated in the renaming of the street is not surprising, given his central significance to the political and commemorative culture of the new state.

★★★

Great Brunswick Street, significantly amended and developed in the nineteenth century (no doubt assisted by the first railway line in Ireland at Westland Row), truly came into its own in the early years of the twentieth century. Two of its defining residents, the emergency services of Dublin Fire Brigade and the police force, took up residence in striking buildings a stone's throw from one another.

Approaching Pearse Street from College Green, or D'Olier Street, the police station immediately grabs the eye. To us, it is Pearse Street Garda Station, but once it was home to the Dublin Metropolitan Police and the much feared G Division, the division of the police which specialised in political intelligence. It was the G Men who identified the leaders of the Easter Rising from the tired and shivering men crowded into the gymnasium of Richmond Barracks after the fighting was over.

Built in a fine Scottish Baronial style, the building was designed by Martin Joseph Burke and Harold Graham Leask and opened in 1915. Sitting at the point where Townsend Street and Great Brunswick Street met, the imposing building contained the G Men's 'Movement of Extremist' files. Conspicuous in their presence on the edge of political demonstrations, or standing at the back of meeting halls, notebook in hand, the police intended to infiltrate, disrupt and observe all who posed a threat to the existing social order.

Today, the Dublin Metropolitan Police may be gone, but officers and constables of the DMP remain, carved into its exterior. They are at two different entrance doors. There is diversity not only in the headgear of the

225

DMP men depicted, but in other features too, like their attire. We can think of them, as Garda Stephen Moore notes in his history of the building, as being, 'indicative of a hierarchy that also stretched inside the building, where administration and budgeting systems, stairs and dormitories, and even the central heating systems were distinct from each other.'[4]

The nineteenth-century G Man was primarily concerned with Fenian radicals, but in the early twentieth century they had a significantly broader range of radicals to watch. There were the socialist Larkinites, those loyal to Liberty Hall, not far from the station across Butt Bridge. There were radical Suffragettes, the window breakers and pioneering hunger strikers. Above all else, though, there were 'advanced nationalists' – those, like Pearse, who dreamt of insurrection.

The name G Man sounds mysterious, though there is little mystery to it, for G is the seventh letter of the alphabet and these men formed the seventh division of the Dublin Metropolitan Police.

There were six physical divisions when it came to policing the Dublin Metropolitan area, A–F. The policemen who worked in Great Brunswick Street were 'the gentlemen of B', and most of their policing was the standard fare of a metropolis. In his entertaining history of policing Victorian Dublin, with the intriguing subtitle 'Mad Dogs, Duels and Dynamite', Barry Kennerk describes how:

Policemen were issued with badge numbers that matched their division, and when they were on duty, they were not supposed to walk at more than three miles an hour so that they could be of most help to members of the public. Strolling at this measured regulation pace, they covered about ten miles per day and got to know all the characters and buildings of note in their areas.[5]

The affable Dublin policeman was nearly always remembered as tall; the minimum height for the DMP was five feet nine inches. This was a full inch taller than the required height of a member of the Royal Irish Constabulary, the force which policed most of the island of Ireland.[6] Some became recognised characters in the life of the city. There was Constable Patrick Sheahan, for example, who had wrestled with an escaped bull on Grafton Street in 1904. The year in which Joyce set *Ulysses*, it's the kind of story not even his mind could conjure up. *The Irish Times* told readers that, 'a large roam bullock which escaped from its keeper, between six and seven o'clock last evening, while being driven along Harcourt Street, created quite a scare in the locality, and before it was finally captured and slaughtered in the vicinity of Grafton Street, after a prolonged struggle with several policemen, it injured two persons, who were subsequently removed to hospital.'[7]

On that occasion, a twenty-minute tangle with the animal witnessed two DMP men utilising a rope to essentially 'lasso' the bull, later calling on butcher Martin

Tierney, who removed it to an abattoir It was a sad end for the bull, but made a familiar face of Constable Sheahan in the city. Sheahan, with great bravado, was reported to have said, 'the only thing I was afraid of was that his horns might break.'[8]

Sheahan met his own death, not far from the police station in which he worked, on 6 May 1905. On that occasion he had bravely gone into the sewers of Dublin to rescue workmen who had succumbed to toxic sewer gas. Sheahan's memorial on Burgh Quay is a reminder of the complexities of the Dublin Metropolitan Police, as it includes an inscription *as Gaeilge*. There was no politics to it; Sheahan was simply a hero to the city. The *Irish Independent* reported after his passing on an occasion in which a Townsend Street house, 'was tumbling into ruins the constable dashed in, and saved an old man and his wife from a terrible death, carrying them out to safety on his brawny shoulders.'[9] The event even inspired a song, *The Burgh Quay Sad Calamity*. Doggerel over ten verses, one will here suffice, naming some of those who rushed to the scene:

And then rushed Mr. Rochford, who showed no sign of fear
Who knew the danger of the place, he being an engineer.
And next comes Patrick Sheahan, a hero of renown
A member of the DMP from good old Limerick town.[10]

Still, within a few short years Sheahan would feel like a folk hero from a different time entirely. The chaos of the 1913 Lockout, the bitter and prolonged dispute over trade union recognition, led to the Dublin Metropolitan Police being supplemented by members of the Royal Irish Constabulary. Soon after, violent confrontations between locked-out workers and the forces of the law.

Jim Phelan, a colourful character who would later pen some of the great tramping memoirs of the twentieth century, travelling the world and refusing to live within four walls, was a young worker in the Inchicore ironworks when the dispute was on. In his account of the time, *The Name's Phelan*, he described the clashes between the combined police forces and the citizenry, recounting that:

> No other city, this century, has known similar experience. London and Paris, Liverpool and Chicago, San Francisco and Detroit and Sydney, have all known bitter and bloody strikes, fierce clashes between capital and labour. The Irish episode was of an entirely different nature … Law was at an end, destroyed by the bludgeon-bearing officers of the law. In the eyes of the constabulary man, a workman on strike was a maniac homicide.[11]

The locked-out workers came to give as good as they got, Phelan recounting how, 'like practically everyone from the Inchicore ironworks in those days, I carried an

THE REAL STRIKERS

On August 30 and 31 the Dublin Metropolitan Police and the R. I. Constabulary ran " amok " in the City of Dublin. Result: Two men batoned to death and several hundred men, women and children badly beaten, whose ages range from one week to ninety years.

'The Real Strikers' – *The Lepracaun* takes aim at the DMP and RIC in this 1913 cartoon (Courtesy of Dublin City Library and Archive) iron bar in my coat-sleeve.'[12] From the dispute emerged the Irish Citizen Army, a protective force for trade union processions and demonstrations. Phelan recounted it as being, at least in its infancy, a perfect retort: 'an organised force of bludgeon-men.'[13] When the Easter Rising came around, two Dublin Metropolitan Police men were amongst the first to fall in the capital, both shot by the Irish Citizen Army. 1913 had left deep scars.

In Great Brunswick Street police station, things were heating up in other ways too. G Division, those tasked with monitoring subversives – or at least those the state regarded as subversives – were increasingly busy. There were new armed militias and auxiliary bodies to observe: the aforementioned Irish Citizen Army, loyal to Liberty Hall; the Irish Volunteers, a southern rebuke to the Carsonites in Ulster who were so loyal to the British Parliament as to threaten war on it; and Cumann na mBan, a body of Irish womanhood founded to support the latter. All of these organisations produced militants who generated pages and pages of intelligence.

What kind of things were the G Men observing? On 4 April 1916, mere weeks before the Rising, their report tells us that, 'about forty members of the Sinn Féin Volunteers were drilled, without rifles, in the hall at rear of 41 Rutland Square, between 8pm and 10pm.' They watched train stations to observe who was coming and going from the city, and kept a close eye on Thomas J. Clarke's shop.[14]

Some in the G Division shifted allegiances, of course, providing information to the republican cause. Most famously, this included Sergeant Eamon Broy, who allowed Michael Collins into the Great Brunswick Street station on 7 April 1919 to view intelligence files, an event commemorated with a plaque at the station.

It is perhaps fitting that this plaque is somewhat hidden, and that most will miss it at the rear door of the station. It befits the secretive nature of the place – and of Broy's heroic act. Broy recounted that, 'G Men were selected from the uniformed service, from those who had at least three years' service in uniform and consequently understood the organisation and working of the uniformed service.' To his mind, the turning point was Easter Week: 'Executions began to take place and, when continued day after day, began to shock and stun a good many of the police and detectives. Death was in the air and young men had been shot as prisoners in Kilmainham Jail.' Broy, working within the G Division and undermining it, was a vital part of the intelligence war.[15]

Other G Men, those who were regarded as a hindrance and not a help, were targeted by the Irish Republican Army. James Slattery, a member of 'The Squad', a tight-knit group of assassins that reported directly to Michael Collins and later played the leading role in the high drama on the morning of Bloody Sunday in November 1920, recounted the shooting of Detective Daniel Hoey on 12 September 1919. It occurred at a time when the republican

A well-hidden plaque to Broy's espionage (Luke Fallon)

movement was under increasing pressure from the intelligence services, and Hoey was labelled as 'the leading spirit in the raiders'. Together with Mick McDonnell, another member of The Squad, Slattery set out to eliminate Hoey, a dramatic night of following the professional follower in the shadows, and which culminated with a degree of luck for the Squad members:

> Hoey crossed over from College Street towards the police headquarters in Brunswick Street. I asked Mick if he was sure that this man was Hoey, and he said, 'I am not quite sure, but we will go after him'.
>
> We intended that if he went straight to the door of the building we would shoot him, but instead of going there he went down Townsend Street nearly as far as Tara Street. We passed him by when he was looking at a window and Mick said, 'It is Hoey all right'. He went into a shop and we passed back up to the corner of Hawkins Street. When we saw him approaching again, we crossed over to his side of the street, which was at the back of the barracks, and we shot him at the door of the garage.[16]

In time, the police station – which was initially known as College Station after independence – would come to carry the name of Pearse, one of the so-called 'extremists' that the DMP took an active interest in.

Sometimes, these revolutionaries were hiding in plain sight and close proximity. At the almost neighbouring Central Fire Station, for example, firefighter Joe Connolly would walk off the job on 24 April 1916 to participate in the Easter Rising with the Irish Citizen Army. In the subsequent revolutionary period, Joe utilised the resources of the Dublin Fire Brigade in pursuit of the aims of the republican movement, moving men and munitions through police cordons in ambulances unlikely to be checked at cordons.[17]

★★★

Though part and parcel of the fabric of Pearse Street, the Central Fire Station is known as Tara Street Fire Station, reflecting its postal address. Opening in 1907, it is one of a number of fine red-brick stations designed by City Architect C. J. McCarthy in the early years of the twentieth century. McCarthy worked closely with Chief Officer Thomas Purcell, a trained engineer, who influenced not only the design of the stations but their locations. Purcell was the great moderniser of the Dublin Fire Brigade, and designed a turntable ladder for use in firefighting which he patented and which proved popular in fire brigades across the neighbouring island. DFB historian Las Fallon has noted that Purcell, 'lies in Deansgrange Cemetery under a headstone built to his own design. In memory of his native place his imposing headstone is made from Kilkenny limestone.'[18]

The watch-tower on the Tara Street elevation is one of the defining architectural features of the local area. An early picture of men working at the station immediately draws our eyes to their brass helmets and motor vehicle, but closer inspection reveals two women standing on the stairwells; in the infancy of the station, firefighters lived with their wives and children in quarters.

While the Dublin Fire Brigade came into being in 1862, under the name Dublin Fire Department, the story of firefighting in the city stretches back much further. For as long as there have been cities, they have had to contend with fire. Indeed, Dublin had to contend with the serious risk of fire from medieval times, with large parts of Dublin destroyed by fire in 1190 and 1283. The course of Dublin's history and development has often been significantly shaped by the city of London, and this was true of The Great Fire of London in September 1666, a fire which historians Tom Geraghty and Trevor Whitehead described as, 'the catalyst for a new era of organised fire fighting.'[19] In subsequent years emerged a primitive fire service, something heralded in 1711 in a dramatic public notice.

Pearse Street occupies an important place in the Dublin Fire Brigade's history, not only as the home of the Central Fire Station, but as the site of tragedy in October 1936, when a blaze at Exide Batteries, 164 Pearse Street, claimed the lives of three firefighters. Peter McArdle,

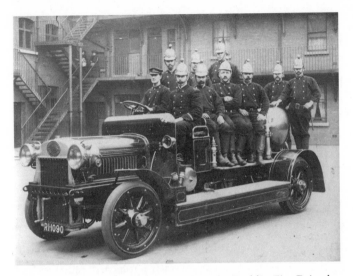

An early crew of the Dublin Fire Brigade (Dublin Fire Brigade Museum)

Robert Malone and Thomas Nugent all left behind grieving families and, in McArdle's case, seven children. Malone was a veteran of the Easter Rising, while Nugent was engaged to be married. Tommy Potts, distinguished traditional musician who would go on to produce the defining LP *The Liffey Banks*, was blown from the roof but somehow survived.

The funerals of the three brought Dublin city to a standstill, Tony Behan writing of how, 'the remains of Fireman Malone were borne on a fire engine from Tara Street, the coffin wrapped in the Tricolour, surrounded by a guard of twenty men who had served with him in Boland's Mill.'[20] A plaque on the Science Gallery of Trinity College Dublin commemorates the three lives lost, and the worst loss of life the Dublin Fire Brigade has endured.

★★★

Opposite the fire station, the Queen's Theatre has disappeared without trace, demolished in 1975. Previously known as the Adelphi, the Queen's came down without much fuss – actor and entertainer Ben Bono standing outside it after its closure with a placard reading 'NO ONE CAME TO THE QUEEN'S FUNERAL'. He told the *Sunday Independent* that, 'she died without a whimper from anybody, so I decided to make a token protest myself.'[21] It was, in fact, the second incarnation of a theatre on the site, as an 1846 guide to Dublin commented on its recent renovation: 'Though small, it is handsomely fitted up, and very well suited for the purposes of the minor drama.'[22]

The Queen's didn't only give its customers 'minor drama', it gave them nationalist heroics in abundance. There were plays telling the life story of men like Robert Emmet and Theobald Wolfe Tone, and plays like Hubert O'Grady's *The Fenian*. In the words of one historian, it all amounted to a 'mythical land of blarney and blather, peopled by patriotic heroes of exclusively aristocratic

THe **LORD MAYOR**, to prevent the Calamities that may happen by Fire, has Ordered Publick Notice to be given,

That *John Oates*, WATER-INGINEER to the Honourable City of *DUBLIN*, living in *Dame-ſtreet* at the Sign of the Boot, is directed by his LORDSHIP to aſſiſt with Two *Water-Ingines* on the firſt Notice that ſhall be given him, when any Fire breaks out in this City or Suburbs.

☞ Note, *That the ſaid* John Oates *makes all Sorts of* Water-Ingines *at Reaſonable Rates, and to as great Perfection as in* London, *baving already made One for the Honourable CITY of* DUBLIN.

Printed by *John Ray* in *Skinner-Row*, Printer to the Honourable City of DUBLIN, 1711.

1711 notice issued by the Lord Mayor (Courtesy of Dublin City Library and Archive)

descent, betrayed by villainous informers and mourned by impossibly innocent colleens'.[23] Not that those who attended the Queen's would care what the reviewers of their age, or the historians of ours, thought of the fare on offer. There was always an enthusiastic audience. The theatre fused historical drama with pantomime-like elements, the crowds booing and hissing performers.

After fire gutted parts of the Abbey Theatre in July 1951 (it was not, as Frank McDonald rightly tells us, 'destroyed by fire') the national theatre embarked on a journey across the city, before settling for a period in the Queen's. Some urged a restoration of the old site rather than the construction of an entirely new theatre, the *Irish Builder* feeling that, 'tourists who come here would prefer to see the old Abbey, the Abbey of Yeats and Synge, rather than the Abbey of Scott.'[24] Nonetheless, a new premises for the national theatre was built, and the Queen's filled the void until it was ready. It was constructed by Michael Scott (and Partners), one of the most significant architects of the Irish twentieth century. Scott's work includes the celebrated Busáras, but the Abbey had a special place in his heart, as an occasional Abbey actor in his youth who had appeared on stage there in the work of O'Casey and others.

Two little boys who grew up on the other side of Great Brunswick Street from the Queen's had great interest in theatre from a young age. In their house, 'Patrick wrote plays performed with cardboard figures against scenery drawn by Patrick and set up by Willie.'[25] Whether the Pearse family attended the Queen's Theatre is something we can only speculate on, though it was within view of their front door.

The restoration of the front of Pearse & Sons at 27 Pearse Street demonstrates the attention to detail of Dublin Civic Trust, which has restored a number of historic buildings and shop fronts across the city. Of 27 Pearse Street, now home to The Ireland Institute, the Trust has described the building:

> Rising three storeys over basement with an elegant red brick façade, finely proportioned sash windows and a railed frontage to the basement well, it typifies the modest scale of buildings erected for an emerging middle class in the opening decades of the 19th century.[26]

James Pearse was perhaps an unlikely father for two Easter Week martyrs – a Unitarian raised in England's Birmingham. Pearse specialised in ecclesiastical and architectural sculputures, and work by his hand and firm can still be seen across the city. Some of the finest surviving James Pearse work is at the Church of St. Augustine and St. John, better known as John's Lane Church, in the heart of the Liberties. There, the twelve statues in the niches of the exterior of the church are his work. For someone who was not himself Catholic, he certainly had an impact on the iconography of Dublin's churches, Patrick later commenting:

> If ever in an Irish church you find, amid a wilderness of bad sculpture, something good and true and lovingly finished you may be sure that it was carved by my father or by one of his pupils.[27]

James Pearse, together with his wife Margaret, created a home in which his children were encouraged to learn and to be creative. There was Shakespeare, Dickens, a Koran, books on Christianity, Freemasonry, Irish history in abundance and numerous volumes on art history and practice. It nurtured intellectual curiosity in the children, and Willie would follow his father by becoming a sculptor, studying at the Metropolitan School of Art under the guidance of Oliver Sheppard. Some of Willie's work is available to view in the Pearse Museum at Rathfarnham, an institution that does much to discredit the idea of Patrick Pearse as some sort of zealot, or inward-looking cultural nationalist with little sense of the broader world.[28]

We can only ponder if Patrick Pearse attended the Queen's Theatre, but it is a matter of historical record that he spoke in the Antient Concert Hall, located at 52 Great Brunswick Street. In journeying to it we pass below the railway bridge, and continue past St Mark's Church, travelling in the opposite direction of Joyce's protagonists in *Ulysses*, who, 'went past the bleak pulpit of saint Mark's [*sic*], under the railway bridge, past the Queen's theatre: in silence.'[29] St Mark's, consecrated on the day of its namesake in April 1757, is the oldest building on Pearse Street.

One of the more curious buildings on the street, the Antient Concert Rooms began life as part of the Dublin Oil Gas Company, which opened here in 1824. The front of the building is still recognisable from John Connolly's depiction of that same year, even if the rest of the scene (goats in the city, a top hat wearing gentleman on horse) is unimaginable.

From 1843, the gas station was reborn as the Antient Concert Rooms. A notice in the newspapers of 20 April 1843 asked, 'that all parties attending the Oratorio ... will proceed by Brunswick Street, in order that the carriages may set down with the horses' heads towards Westland Row.' This being Dublin, and its centenary then fresh in the memory, it seems fitting that a performance of Handel's *Messiah* launched the venue.[30] The venue succeeded in attracting international talent, like the great Jenny Lind, recalled as 'the Swedish Nightingale'. Lind's performance in 1859 is recalled in a study of the venue as 'the greatest event in the history of the Rooms.'[31]

Opera, in time, gave way to the Irish cultural revival. Before the establishment of the Abbey Theatre, the Antient Concert Rooms hosted plays by the Irish Literary Theatre, the nucleus of what was to come. There

John Connolly's 1824 illustration of the Dublin Oil Gas Company
premises (National Library of Ireland)

were performances of works like *The Countess Cathleen*
(1899) by William Butler Yeats, as well as work by Lady
Gregory and Edward Martyn. Later, the first president of
Sinn Féin, Martyn is a curiously forgotten figure in the
cultural and political life of the nation.

The content brought to the stage by the Abbey
Theatre, like John Millington Synge's *The Playboy of the
Western World* in 1907, would sometimes lead to real
controversy. Some sought an idealised Ireland on stage,
perhaps more accustomed to the heroic tales of the
Queen's Theatre. There were signs of what was to come
for the Abbey in its earliest days at the Antient Concert

Rooms however, Lady Gregory recounting the hostility in some quarters to *The Countess Cathleen*, a play in which a woman sells her soul to the devil, to save the lives of her starving tenants. Gregory recalled that:

> Some rough and ready theologians saw fit to object to the suggestion that God had forgiven a woman who so far forgot her duty, intimating it as a reflection upon the doctrines of Catholic orthodoxy. Their banding together to break up the performances, interfered with by the police who acted in the interests of law and order, really made thinking people wonder what time of day it is with certain people in Ireland.[32]

In the fusing of the cultural and political causes which were gripping the city, Yeats and Pearse shared a plat-form in the Antient Concert Rooms in November 1914, at an event honouring the centenary year of the birth of the poet and separatist Thomas Davis. One of those in the room that night was the poet Austin Clarke, still a teenager. He remembered that Yeats quoted Nietzsche, shocking to the audience, 'for the German poet and philosopher of the Superman was regarded with horror in all our pro-British press dur-ing the First World War.' Pearse spoke next, and Clarke tells us, 'I had only heard vaguely of him ... Pearse spoke with an intense lofty devotion which stirred me

245

uneasily for it was a cold, impassioned rhetoric which was new to me, and carefully declaimed.' There was another speaker, who arrived late to proceedings, in the form of Captain Thomas Kettle, 'braving us in the uniform of a British Officer. He marched up the hall so firmly that we almost seemed to hear the clatter of his sword but it was obvious that he had his fill of Irish whiskey in order that he might defy more confidently this small group of Sinn Féiners.'[33]

Kettle had followed the parliamentary leader John Redmond in encouraging Irishmen to enlist in the European War, a decision which would cost him his own life at the Somme in 1916. Pearse, by then, was dead too. Only Yeats would live to see an Irish Free State.

The shouting match that consumed the hall, and the hecklers who mocked Kettle's new uniform, would all be forgotten. The final words on the venue go to Austin Clarke:

When the meeting was over and I came out, I saw W. B. Yeats surrounded by disciples and watched the group walking towards Westland Row. The next morning the placards appeared with the startling announcement: *Dublin audience cheers Nietzsche.*[34]

Much has changed on Pearse Street since the crowd walked out of the Antient Concert Rooms that night. Whatever G Man stood at the door, or across the street, watching for familiar faces would likely be surprised to learn that while the police station would remain a century later, the Dublin Metropolitan Police is now a historical memory. The 'extremists' won the day.

12

Moore Street

A 1978 view of Moore Street (Courtesy of Dublin City Library and Archive)

The story of any publication is not just that within its pages, but the context in which it was written and published. Has the recent pandemic, or the housing crisis, shaped how this very book interpreted the past? Undoubtedly, it influenced the inclusion of Church Street, to which the story of the 1914 Housing Inquiry is key, and on a more personal level it inspired the inclusion of Rathmines Road Lower, a street that revealed its layers to me on lockdown walks.

Perhaps there is no better example of a book shaped by its time than Flora Mitchell's *Vanishing Dublin*, published in 1966. Against the backdrop of a rapidly changing city, Flora – a graduate of the Metropolitan School of Art who was born 'under wide skies on the cattle ranges of Western America' – set out to capture a city she had fallen in love with. In pencil and watercolour brush, she gave us Dublin as it appeared before her.

In the year of the appearance of *Vanishing Dublin*, one architect proclaimed, 'that part of the city to which we refer as Georgian Dublin has long outlived its life expectancy.'[1] A few years later, those who protested to save the built heritage of the city were denounced in the Dáil as 'a consortium of belted earls and their ladies and left-wing intellectuals'.[2] The collapse of several tenements in the city in 1963, following a period of abnormal weather conditions which tested the fabric of the city, was one catalyst for demolition in the city. Much more was done at the whim of developers. The writer John Ryan captured the feeling of many, telling the *Irish Independent,* 'I am never opposed to progress, but I will fight to defend the beautiful.'[3]

The fear of Mitchell, as she expressed it, was her sense that, 'to walk in Dublin brings the realisation that soon it must become just another city of concrete and glass, colourless and stereotyped.'[4] When we flick through her book there are place names that now sound like answers in a Dublin table quiz: Horseman's Row, Paradise Court, Derby Court.

Other names are more familiar, including Moore Street. She tells us:

> In the days when this was the fashionable quarter of Dublin, here was the main shopping district, but gradually it became an open market, radiating out into courts and lanes filled with booths and stalls. Moore Street today suffers from periodic threatening of closure, but much trading is done here, and the street is a riot of colour and noise.[5]

Reading of 'periodic threatening of closure' is a reminder that Moore Street has long been in a state of paralysis.

It's interesting to think of the author as someone in search of the authentic Dublin (if such a thing could even exist), and who in doing so was drawn to Moore Street and streets like it. Similarly, Kevin Corrigan Kearns found himself there in search of something truly of this place.

'Better stalls mean better business' – Dublin Corporation proposed
stand for Moore Street traders, 1959 (Courtesy of Dublin City
Library and Archive)

An American cultural geographer from the University
of Northern Colorado, Kearns would emerge from the
late 1980s and early 1990s as the most important oral
historian of the city, perhaps blessed with the comfort
of distance, not so familiar to those he interviewed
that they wouldn't open themselves fully. As Kearns
recounted in his ground-breaking *Dublin Street Life &*

Lore: An Oral History, Dublin offered a whole variety of fascinating characters in the twentieth century, 'figures such as lamplighters, buskers, jarveys, newspaper sellers, dockers, drovers, dealers and spielers who have contributed to the exuberance and drama of the streets.'[6] For him, there was an allure to Moore Street. May Mooney, a Moore Street trader, told him:

> Me mother sold and me two aunties sold and me grandmother sold. I was in it from a child. The women who were dealers, their daughters took over from them. It was tradition. The generations … tradition, tradition.[7]

Moore Street takes its name from developer Henry Moore, Earl of Drogheda, who with typical modesty proceeded to name it and just about everywhere else around it after himself. Henry Street, Moore Street, North Earl Street, Drogheda Street (later absorbed into what eventually became our main thoroughfare) and even Of Lane ensured that wherever else he may be forgotten, his name would live eternally on a map of Dublin.

Séamus Scully, a resident of Moore Street over many decades who wrote much on the street, has left us a lot of research on the development of the street, as well as his own first-hand recollections of the Easter Rising, which played out before his horrified eyes. At the age of eighty-one, his research was published in *The Dublin Rover*, an enjoyable read with an introduction lamenting that, 'some historians impose themselves on their subjects, on the locales, and issue solemn nostrums from the dung-heaps of their arrogance.'[8] Séamus wrote of what, and who, he knew. In 'Ghosts of Moore Street', he described the early history of the street and those who took up residence there. They were men and women of privileged means, like Benjamin Higgins, who placed a notice in the pages of the *Freeman's Journal* in September 1719 lamenting his disappearing servant: 'As he was easy tempered, it is supposed he was wheeled away by some evil-minded person … He is about 16 years old, marked with small-pox, with light hair and tender eyes.'[9] We don't know if he returned.

As a market street, Moore Street began to flourish in the second half of the eighteenth century, reflecting the progress of the city more broadly. Barry Kennerk, author of a loving history of the street, suggests a variety of factors for this, like, 'the increasing cost of rent on Henry Street, which caused grocers to migrate into the adjacent streets where overheads were cheaper.'[10] In a city of emerging streets and squares that catered to the wealthy, markets thrived in providing food for the long tables.

Our sense of Moore Street today is shaped by the dominant presence of the ILAC Shopping Centre. The ILAC, the *Evening Herald* told readers in 1981, 'is so modern in concept that it is virtually tomorrow's world.'[11] Perhaps that says more about Ireland in 1981 than it does the shopping centre. The ILACs footprint takes up what was once a warren of little

1987 image of the ILAC and Moore Street, almost unrecognisable with modern development (Courtesy of Dublin City Library and Archive)

streets and alleys, with forgotten names like Riddall's Row and Horseman's Row.

As the city itself tumbled downwards in the nineteenth century, so did this district, *The Irish Builder and Engineer* of 1861 painting a grim picture of, 'fowl, butchers' meat, fish and vegetables all huddled together in dilapidated stalls … how revolting to decency, how detrimental in a sanitary regard!'[12] Beyond food, some of the lanes specialised in second-hand clothing, others in furniture. This was the tenement economy.

Some four decades after independence, the American town planner Charles Abrams (dispatched to Ireland after the Minister for Local Government requested an expert

Before the ILAC. One of the markets beside Moore Street, 1975
(Courtesy of Dublin City Library and Archive)

from the UN to advise on aspects of the development of the city centre) wrote of these laneways surrounding Moore Street, 'as an exemplar of the problems facing much of the city.'[13] Moore Street had great life, 'an atmosphere of activity amid squalor', but the broader picture he painted was grim:

> There are a number of empty lots as one crosses Riddles Row, while McCann's Lane has a number of old small one-story buildings and a few decrepit two and three story buildings. Contributing to the general drabness are some old slaughterhouses...On weekdays some small scale peddling is done in one of the alleys

255

and there are the push carts on Moore Street with its busy retail shops giving an atmosphere of activity amid squalor...the area is definitely decayed - or as the court put it in 1942, 'part of that area is a dreadful blot on the city, and I welcome the evidence that the Corporation is determined on sweeping reforms in a shocking district.' Eighteen years later, the buildings still stand, older and shabbier than ever.[14]

Moore Street itself, then, as Ambrams and others viewed it, was faring much better than its neighbouring environment. Walking down the street today, there is a sense of strong historical continuity in some businesses, like the business of Francis Xavier Buckley, which opened in the 1930s, promising meat 'Par Excellence'. Mosaic tiles outside F. X. Buckley's depict sheep and cows. There were other family institutions too, like the name Martin & Son over the door of 55 Moore Street. That butchers thrived from the 1930s until the early 1990s. Above 55, a carved stone dragon keeps watch over the street.

★★★

The street attracted mention in many guidebooks to the post-independence city, while in October 1958 the press reported, 'Moore Street was thronged last night for the selecting of 'Molly Malone 1958' from among the street's 100 dealers who wore colourful costumes and hats.'[15] The association of Molly Malone with the street remained into subsequent decades. When the statue was to be moved from Grafton Street in 2013 for the Luas, Councillor Nial Ring suggested she be placed on Moore Street, insisting that, 'the Molly Malone statue is a most appropriate symbol of the rich street trading heritage and Molly should come home.'[16] She never made it across the Liffey.

Molly Malone, a character from the city's folklore and mythology, can come in whatever guise one wants. Comedian Brendan O'Carroll, who championed Moore Street's traders in his film *Mrs Brown's Boys D'Movie*, would speak of how, 'Moore Street is where Molly Malone originally plied her trade. The market stalls are run by tough, hard women, and they have a great turn of phrase, really quick wit.'[17]

If Molly Malone *was* real, would she have found herself in the back of a 1980s Garda van? By then, there were tensions between the largely female street traders of the inner-city and the authorities, driven significantly by the hostility of local businesses to their presence. Much of this concerned unlicensed traders, who banded together under the name of the Molly Malone Association, telling the press:

> The Molly Malone Association has sixty members, many of whom have traded in the streets for the last twenty to forty years. Over the years we have

been constantly moved by the Gardaí and fined for illegal trading … We are ordinary women trying to keep a roof over our heads and food on our tables by continuing our families' tradition of street trading. It is our only income. We are fed up with being victimised for trying to earn an honest living.[18]

By then, Molly's old cart was a memory, Kennerk writing of, 'the appearance of the Silver Cross pram with a breadboard slung across it.'[19] Joe Lee, an independent filmmaker who has made some beautiful social history documentaries about the city, titled a documentary on the markets district of Dublin called *Bananas on the Breadboard*.[20]

Both Christy Burke, a local councillor from Sinn Féin, and independent TD Tony Gregory were veterans of the republican movement, but found themselves fighting battles closer to home in the Dublin of the 1980s, including for these unlicensed traders. Their involvement in anti-drugs activism had brought both much respect in the inner city, where heroin was a much greater concern to residents than unlicensed trading from prams. Gregory had succeeded in winning an unprecedented level of funding for inner-city communities and facilities by giving his support to Charles Haughey following the 1982 General Election which failed to return an overall majority. Following one 1985 protest where street traders blocked O'Connell Street, Gregory and Burke

The late Tony Gregory speaking in City Hall. Beside him is
Christy Burke (Courtesy of Dublin City Library and Archive)

were both arrested and sentenced to two weeks imprisonment. A *Sunday Press* report, from the aftermath of
Gregory's imprisonment, gives a sense of the adoration
for him from traders:

> The flower and trinket sellers of Henry Street and
> Moore Street marched on Mountjoy Jail last night
> to show their solidarity with their imprisoned TD,
> Tony Gregory.

> They pushed their prams from O'Connell Street to
> the jail, disturbing traffic on the way and chanting
> 'We want Tony! Free Tony Gregory!'

> They were furious with the authorities for allowing the imprisonment. One remarked: 'They allow the drug pushers out but send Tony to prison for defending our right to work.'[21]

Gregory was just 61 at the time of his passing in 2009. Despite many years spent in Kildare Street, it was another street which appeared most frequently in his obituaries. In the *Irish Independent*, readers were told 'his causes were numerous. He became a felon for defending the Moore Street traders.'[22]

The Moore Street traders, like Moore Street itself, have a very secure past. There are considerably more questions around the future. Róisín Curé, an 'urban sketcher' who draws life in the city as she sees it, described the street with frank honesty in her recent publication *Dublin in Sketches and Stories*. To her, 'the row of stalls with their royal-blue and white striped canopies is inspiring,' but there is also very real urban decay and a sense of neglect, of both buildings and people: 'Unfortunate souls to whom life has not been kind seem to be everywhere.'[23]

The street still has tremendous personalities, many from new communities who have sought to establish businesses there. On a walk down it one can sample Brazilian Coxinha or Pão de queijo, Indian biryani and even Àkàrà, a tasty bean cake originating in Nigeria. Yet despite this vibrancy there is a sense of limbo, with little permanence to these new businesses as the future of the street is contested.

At the heart of the Moore Street issue is the connection of the street itself, and its surrounding laneways that survive behind its terrace, to the Easter Rising.

The Rising conjures up images of the blazing General Post Office. In Neil Jordan's *Michael Collins*, it is the GPO from which the headquarters garrison of the insurrection surrenders. The defining artistic representation of the Rising, later reinterpreted by Robert Ballagh, is Walter Paget's *Birth of the Irish Republic,* in which the building itself is as much a character to the work as Pearse, Connolly and others depicted. Originally an imperial building, constructed by Francis Johnston (who also designed the neighbouring Nelson's Pillar), 'it is now a symbol, if not *the* symbol, of Irish independence as headquarters of the 1916 nationalist fighters and the site of their accompanying proclamation of independence.'[24]

The Easter Rising may have begun with the declaration of a republic at the pillars of the GPO, but the decision to surrender was ultimately taken on Moore Street, following the abandonment of the Post Office on the fifth day of the insurrection. Getting to Moore Street involved frantic dashes into the laneways of Henry Place and Moore Lane. Desmond Ryan, speaking with a vividness and pace that recalls his career as a writer, told the Bureau of Military History:

IRISH REBELLION, MAY 1916.

THE O'RAHILLY.
One of the Leaders, who was Snot in Act on, G.P.O. Area.

The O'Rahilly, killed in the evacuation of the General Post Office
(Courtesy of Dublin City Library and Archive)

Signage for a memorial to The O'Rahilly on Moore Street
(Luke Fallon)

We dash across the flame lit and bullet swept street, up Henry Place, into stables, down sombre alleys lighted by machine gun fire. The bullets patter upon the walls. Men fall. Plunkett rallies the men past a bullet swept barricade. Connolly has been borne on a stretcher to Moore Street beneath a red-cross flag. O'Rahilly outdistances his men and a machine-gun riddles him within a few yards of the barricade.[25]

There is something both heroic and tragic in the story of The O'Rahilly, who had opposed the insurrection and actively worked to stop it from becoming a reality in the days before it commenced, but who ultimately took his place in the fight. His beautiful French De Dion-Bouton sports car had met its own end on a rebel barricade. Dublin lore has it that O'Rahilly's car ended up under Croke Park's Hill 16, which was supposedly built from the rubble of the city. Sports historian Paul Rouse has done much to dismantle this myth, writing that 'it appears that this myth was first aired in the 1930s', with a letter to a newspaper ahead of the 1939 All Ireland Final noting that the blood of Ireland's fallen heroes 'stains the debris in that immortal hill'.[26] The Hill, alas, predated the Rising. More peculiarly, it had been known as Hill 60, in honour of a battle in the First World War.

While O'Rahilly's car may not be below the Hill, his departing words are eternally part of the streetscape around Moore Street, with a plaque on neighbouring O'Rahilly Parade. Sculpted by Shane Cullen, it reproduces not only the words of O'Rahilly but his handwriting:

Written after I was shot –
Darling Nancy
I was shot leading a rush up Moore Street
took refuge in a doorway.
While I was there I heard the men pointing out
where I was & I made a bolt for the lane I am in now.
I got more one bullet I think
Tons & tons of love dearie to you & to the boys &
to Nell & Anna.

It was a good fight anyhow.
Please deliver this to Nannie O'Rahilly
40 Herbert Park
Dublin
Good bye darling

For the majority of the GPO garrison, the end of the Rising played out in a Moore Street terrace. Having eventually succeeded in entering the houses, they proceeded to 'mouse-hole' through the block, a tactic they had been taught by James Connolly before the Rising. Obsessed with historical urban fighting, Connolly had studied events like the 1871 Paris Commune in meticulous detail. To his mind, it made no sense to tunnel through a row of buildings at the same level, and he advised moving through various levels for the protection it offered should enemy forces enter the same block.[27] Séamus Kavanagh, a member of the Irish Volunteers, recounted that 'I felt very sorry for the people who lived in these houses. By going into them we were bringing death and destruction to the inhabitants'.[28]

Séamus Scully, then a young inhabitant of the street where this drama was unfolding, recalled the traumatic experiences of his neighbours. The names are unfamiliar to us, but Scully captures the feeling of a community in panic, as people zig-zagged in and out of the chaos trying to find safety:

M ouse at No. 59, with a white flag in hand, was shot dead. On the roadway lay stretched Mr and Mrs Dillon with their daughter from No. 8. Now, the Doyle and McDonagh families, tenants at No.16, feared that the chemist shop – Gore's, beside them would catch fire and decided that they must try and seek safety with their friends in the opposite lane. Mr Doyle attached his wife's apron to an umbrella followed by seven others (one carrying a child), they dashed out to the roadway: immediately they were sprayed with bullets.[29]

The end of the Rising has been well documented. In the company of Elizabeth O'Farrell, who had bravely gone to the British barricade before him to inquire as to the possibility of negotiating, Patrick Henry Pearse made his way towards General William Lowe. Scully describes him:

In his heavy military overcoat and Boer-shaped hat he marched down towards the barricade; the nurse almost trotting by his side. Here he was received by General Lowe, to whom he handed his word, pistol and ammunition, also his tin canteen which contained two large onions. On the footpath, outside of Byrne's shop on the corner of Moore Street and Parnell Street, an old wooden bench, which was used for displaying pickled pigs heads, was brought out from the shop; here Pearse stopped and signed the document of surrender which had been placed on it.[30]

A hostile contemporary take on the Easter Rising from the American press. Notice the rifle, 'Made in Germany' (Library of Congress)

The Rising transformed the appearance of Moore Street in other places too. Flames had taken hold in the area early in the uprising, as looters set fire to premises on nearby Henry Street. The widespread looting that gripped the city reflected the abysmal poverty of so many. It is telling that the first shops emptied were not those selling luxury goods, but shoe shops. An example of the reborn street is Number 2 Moore Street, a terraced four-bay three-storey building, which was built in 1917 as the city was re-emerging. The architect Francis Bergin was kept busy, not only on Moore Street but neighbouring Henry Street, North Earl Street, O'Connell Street and Abbey Street.

Buildings reconstructed entirely in the aftermath of the Rising
(Luke Fallon)

Easter Week is forever part of the story of Moore Street, and no telling of the rebellion is complete without the place of that market street in it. There are competing visions of a Moore Street for the future, while also being general agreement that the street requires revitalisation. Campaigners maintain that this is possible while preserving the battlefield sites of the Rising.

There is much else in Moore Street that requires preservation, and even revitalisation. Today, fewer than twenty stall holders work on the street. In the days of the multinational supermarket (one of which is to be found on Moore Street), the manner in which we buy food has been radically transformed, but is there scope for some kind of market to prosper on Moore Street once more? And those who have brought the world to Moore Street, by taking a chance on an area with a precarious future and little security of tenure, must be included too.

Acknowledgements

This book was written in a city emerging from a pandemic which had far-reaching impacts on almost every aspect of life here.

It is a credit to our cultural institutions that many remarkable collections of historic materials have been made publicly accessible, allowing greater and more democratic interaction with the past. In a time when our cultural institutions were greatly restricted in terms of interactions with the public and researchers, there was unprecedented access to historic materials in the public domain.

I am indebted to:

Tara Doyle, Brendan Teeling and all at the Dublin City Library and Archive. The DCLA are truly committed to the promotion of history in the city. I would encourage all readers of this book to seize on the brilliant offerings of their local library. The Royal Irish Academy for providing free public access to the invaluable Dictionary of Irish Biography. The National Archives of Ireland for the digitisation of historic census returns, Dublin Metropolitan Police intelligence files and more. The National Gallery of Ireland for their bold decision to make hundreds of works available freely under Creative Commons for reuse. The National Library of Ireland for their digitisation of materials, some of which are reprinted in this work. Military Archives for hosting the Bureau of Military History Witness Statements, the Military Service Pension Collection and more besides. JStor, a digital library which has served researchers for a quarter of a century, which responded to the pandemic by allowing free access to one hundred articles monthly to all users.

I believe that these institutions and others like them are performing a public good in increasingly looking towards making materials accessible to the largest possible audience.

My thanks to Eibhlin Colgan, archivist at Guinness. Thanks also to all at the Dublin City Council Culture Company, at Richmond Barracks and 14 Henrietta Street. For valuable insights into different aspects of Dublin's history, I thank artist Robert Ballagh, folklorist and oral historian Terry Fagan and Dublin 8 authority Cathy Scufill. I am indebted to designer Paul Guinan, not only for friendship but for his excellent work on the initial branding of *Three Castles Burning* and his work on podcast merchandise.

On a personal level, I wish to thank my partner, Sarah Rochford, for her unending support and love. Thanks to all of the Rochford family in Waterford.

Eternal thanks to my parents, Las and Maria Fallon, who instilled a great love of the city of Dublin in me. I am proud of the contributions of both to improving the lives of others and to serving the people of the city. The important work of Las on the history of the Dublin Fire Brigade influenced this book in places.

My brother, Luke Fallon, took many of the contemporary images of the city in this work. I thank him for his commitment and for his great observations on Dublin. It was a real privilege to utilise the camera of our late uncle, Joe Fallon, which added enormously to this project.

I wish to thank colleagues, in particular Tommy Graham of Historical Insights/*History Ireland*, who has done much to ensure the place of history in the mainstream.

There are many historians to whom I am indebted for friendship. Pádraig Óg Ó Ruairc, Fergus Whelan and Lorcan Collins are some who I find endlessly intriguing. My thanks to all historians, writers and observers of the human condition (from Daniel Lambert on Bang Bang to sportswriter Roy Curtis) who have agreed to come on the podcast and to talk about a city they all clearly love.

Thanks to all at Dublin City Council Culture Company. Thanks to Gavan Reilly at Newstalk, a broadcaster with a keen understanding of the role of history in the contemporary.

Thanks to the family of the late Anthony Behan of the Old Dublin Society for their generous donation of a collection of *Dublin Historical Reviews*, invaluable in writing this book. Tony's presence is greatly missed in the city.

Thanks to the Smith/Kennedy dynasty that still rules South William Street from The Castle Lounge, Willie and all at The Palace, Tommy O'Neill (the upstairs Master of Ceremonies) and all at the Lord Edward. These places are all special in their own ways and part of a dying breed. Thanks to Dara Gannon for access to his images of The Castle Lounge and for his friendship.

Thanks to all friends in Dublin, Belfast, Manchester, Salford, Liverpool, 'Contae London' and Berlin (it was a joy to spend so much time in 2021 in Friedrichsfelde) Particular thanks to Rory Mulvaney in Dublin for his guidance and knowledge in a difficult time.

Thanks to all at New Island Books. It is a pleasure to see their imprint on a book, with a proud history that stretches back to Raven Arts Press. Special thanks to editor Noel O'Regan for bringing much clarity to the text and for tightening the work.

My eternal thanks and gratitude to those who support Three Castles Burning on Patreon. Your support allows the podcast to develop and your support, whether a current subscriber or in the past, is something I am deeply grateful for. In a city where heritage ground to a halt, it would not have been possible to sustain myself and the podcast without you.

Select Bibliography

Archival/Primary Source Materials
1901/1911 Census Returns, National Archives of Ireland
Bureau of Military History Witness Statements, Military Archives
Dublin Corporation Minute Books, Dublin City Library and Archive
Dublin Metropolitan Police Movement of Extremist Files, National Archives of Ireland
Guinness Archive
Irish Left Archive, Cedar Lounge Revolution
Military Service Pensions Collection, Military Archives
Thom's Directory
Unpublished Excavations, The Heritage Council

Newspapers/Periodicals
An Phoblacht
Build
Dublin Historical Record
Evening Herald
Evening Press
Freeman's Journal
History Ireland
Irish Arts Review
Irish Examiner
Irish Independent
Irish Press
Jacobin
Plan

Saothar
Sinn Féin
The Catholic Standard
The Harp
The Irish Times (especially *An Irishman's Diary)*
The Irish Worker
The Lepracaun Cartoon Monthly
The Workers' Republic
Wood Quay Occupation News

Secondary Sources

Ballagh, Robert. *A Reluctant Memoir* (London, 2018)

Bardon, Jonathan. *Hallelujah: The Story of a Musical Genius and the City that brought his Masterpiece to Life* (Dublin, 2015)

Bolger, Dermot (ed.) *Invisible Dublin: A Journey Through Dublin's Suburbs* (Dublin, 1991)

Bradley, John. *Viking Dublin Exposed: The Wood Quay Saga* (Dublin, 1984)

Carden, Sheila. *The Alderman: Alderman Tom Kelly (1868–1942) and Dublin Corporation* (Dublin, 2017)

Collins, Lorcan. *Ireland's War of Independence: 1919–21* (Dublin, 2019)

Craig, Maurice. *Dublin 1660–1860* (Dublin, 1952)

Curtis, Maurice. *Temple Bar: A History* (Dublin, 2016)

Curtis, Maurice. *A Challenge to Democracy: Militant Catholicism in Modern Ireland* (Dublin, 2010)

Daly, Mary E. *Dublin: The Deposed Capital* (Dublin, 1984)

Dickson, David. *Dublin: The Making of a Capital City* (London, 2014)

Fagan, Terry. *Monto: Madams, Murder and Black Coddle* (Dublin, 2000)

Fallon, Las. *Dublin Fire Brigade and the Irish Revolution* (Dublin, 2012)

Geraghty, Tom. Whitehead, Trevor. *The Dublin Fire Brigade* (Dublin, 2004)

Gibney, John. *Dublin: A New Illustrated History* (Dublin, 2017)

Hayes, Melanie. *14 Henrietta Street: Georgian Beginnings, 1750–1800* (Dublin, 2021)

Hopkins, Frank. *Hidden Dublin: Deadbeats, Dossers and Decent Skins* (Dublin, 2008)

Kearns, Kevin C. *Dublin Street Life & Lore: An Oral History* (Dublin, 1991)

Kearns, Kevin C. *Dublin Tenement Life: An Oral History of the Dublin Slums* (Dublin, 2006)

Kennerk, Barry. *Moore Street: The Story of Dublin's Market District* (Cork, 2012)

Harvey, John. *Dublin: A Study in Environment* (London, 1949)

Kilfeather, Siobhán Marie. *Dublin: A Cultural History* (Oxford, 2005)

MacThomáis, Éamonn. *Me Jewel and Darlin' Dublin* (Dublin, 1977)

MacThomáis, Éamonn. *The Labour and the Royal* (Dublin, 1979)

McCready, C. T. *Dublin Street Names: Dated and Explained* (Dublin, 1892)

McDonald, Frank. *A Little History of the Future of Dublin* (Dublin, 2021)

McDonald, Frank. *The Destruction of Dublin* (Dublin, 1985)

McManus, Ruth. *Dublin, 1910–1940: Shaping the City and Suburbs* (Dublin, 2021)

Mitchell, Flora. *Vanishing Dublin* (Dublin, 1966)

Murtagh, Timothy. *14 Henrietta Street: Grandeur and Decline, 1800–1922* (Dublin, 2021)

O'Brien, Joseph. *Dear, Dirty Dublin: A City in Distress, 1899–1916* (California, 1982)

Ó Maitiú, Séamas. *Dublin's Suburban Towns, 1834–1930* (Dublin, 2003)

Pakenham, Thomas. Valerie, Pakenham (eds.). *Dublin: A Traveller's Reader* (London, 2018)

Pearson, Peter. *The Heart of Dublin: Resurgence of an Historic City* (Dublin, 2000)

Pritchett, V. S. *Dublin: A Portrait* (London, 1967)

Scully, Séamus. *The Dublin Rover* (Dublin, 1991)

Simpson, Anne. *Blooming Dublin: Choice, Change and Contradictions* (Dublin, 1991)

Somerville-Large, Peter. *Dublin: The Fair City* (London, 1996)

von Noorden, Djinn (ed.). *Malton's Views of Dublin: The Story of a Georgian City* (Dublin, 2021)

Yeates, Padraig. *A City in Wartime: Dublin 1914–1918* (Dublin, 2012)

Yeates, Padraig. *Lockout: Dublin 1913* (Dublin, 2000)

Ward, Margaret. *Fearless Woman: Hanna Sheeny Skeffington, Feminism and the Irish Revolution* (Dublin, 2019)

Whelan, Fergus. *God-Provoking Democrat: The Remarkable Life of Archibald Hamilton Rowan* (Dublin, 2015)

Endnotes

INTRODUCTION

1   Dermot Bolger (ed.), *Invisible Dublin: A Journey Through Dublin's Suburbs* (Dublin, 1991), p. 15.

1   HENRIETTA STREET

1.   Melanie Hayes, *14 Henrietta Street: Georgian Beginnings 1750–1800* (Dublin, 2021), p. 7.

2.   Edward Casey, resident of 13 Henrietta Street, interviewed in *The Dublin Gazette*, 3 December 2015.

3.   Eugene Hammond, *Jonathan Swift: Irish Blow-In* (Delaware, 2016), p. 334.

4.   John Coleman, 'Luke Gardiner (1745–98): An Irish Dilettante' in *Irish Arts Review Yearbook* (Vol. 15, 1999), pp. 160–68.

5.   Hayes, p. 16.

6.   David Dickson, *Dublin: The Making of a Capital* (London, 2014), p. 300.

7.   Jenny McAuley, 'From the Education of Daughters to the Rights of Women: Mary Wollstonecraft in Ireland, 1786–7', *History Ireland* (Vol. 24, No. 1), pp. 22–25.

8.   William Edward Hartpole Lecky, *A History of Ireland in the Eighteenth Century, Volume 5* (London, 1898), p. 303.

9.   Thomas and Valerie Pakenham, *Dublin: A Traveller's Reader* (Dublin, 2018), p. 19.

10. Timothy Murtagh, *14 Henrietta Street: Grandeur and Decline 1800–1922* (Dublin, 2021), p. 12.

11. *Ibid.*

12. *Ibid.*

13. *Hansard's Parliamentary Debates*, 28 May 1875.

14. Murtagh, p. 25.
15. Gabriella Bennett, 'The trouble with Scotland's tenements and how to lower emissions', *The Times*, 26 October 2021.
16. Kevin C. Kearns, *Dublin Tenement Life: An Oral History of the Dublin Slums* (Dublin, 2006), p. 5.
17. James Joyce, *Dubliners* (London, 1914), p. 150.
18. Donal O'Donovan, *Kevin Barry and His Time* (Dublin, 1989), p. 60.
19. *Ibid*.
20. 'Conor Dodd on Henrietta Street in WWI', Dublin Tenement Experience. Available at: https://dublintenementexperience.wordpress.com/2013/08/23/conor-dodd-on-henrietta-street-men-in-wwi/.
21. Donal Fallon, *14 Henrietta Street: From Tenement to Suburbia* (Dublin, 2021), p. 13.
22. *1913 Report of the Departmental Committee into the Housing conditions of the Working Classes in the City of Dublin* (Dublin, 1914)
23. John Harvey, *Dublin: A Study in Environment* (London, 1949), p. 11.
24. Flora Mitchell, *Vanishing Dublin* (Dublin, 1966), p. 76.
25. *Irish Press*, 19 July 1978.
26. Frank McDonald, *The Destruction of Dublin* (Dublin, 1985), p. 12.
27. Erika Hanna, 'Dublin's North Inner-City, Preservationism, and Irish Modernity in the 1960s', *The Historical Journal* (Vol. 53, No. 4), p. 1028.
28. *Ibid*.
29. Brian McAvera, 'State of Surveillance', *Irish Arts Review* (Vo. 27, No. 1), p. 66.
30. *The Irish Times*, 30 September 2006.
31. *Arts Express*, broadcast on RTÉ 2, February 1990.
32. Fintan O'Toole, introduction to James Plunkett, *Strumpet City* (Dublin, 2013), p. 10.
33. Garrett Fagan, 'Strumpet City: One City One Book', Dublin Tenement Experience, 10 August 2013. Available at: https://dublintenementexperience.wordpress.com/2013/08/10/garrett-fagan-strumpet-city-one-city-one-book/. (Accessed 23 November 2021.)
34. Gaby Wood, 'This Dublin Block Tells the Story of the City', *The New York Times*, 10 September 2018.

2   WATLING STREET

1. Fionn Davenport, *Dublin* (Lonely Planet, 2006), p. 88.
2. Francis Devine introduction to Martin Duffy, *The Trade Union Pint: The Unlikely Union of Guinness and the Larkins* (Dublin, 2012), p. 9.
3. Lar Redmond, *Show Us The Moon* (Kerry, 1988), p. 56.

4. *Dublin Inquirer*, 11 January 2017.
5. Patrick Lynch and John Vaizey, *Guinness's Brewery in the Irish Economy 1759–1876* (Cambridge, 1960), p. 40.
6. *Ibid.*
7. Rob Goodbody, *Irish Historic Town Atlas: Dublin 1756–1847* (Dublin, 2014), p. 4.
8. *Irish Press*, 21 July 1951.
9. Katharine Worth, *Samuel Beckett's Theatre: Life Journeys* (Oxford, 2001), p. 137.
10. Cyril Barrett, 'The Visual Arts and Society, 1921-84' in J. R. Hill (ed.), *A New History of Ireland Volume VII: Ireland, 1921–84* (Oxford, 2003), p. 599.
11. *Irish Independent*, 2 June 1939.
12. For more on Simms see Donal Fallon, 'Tenements, suburbia and the remarkable architect Herbert Simms' in *History on Your Doorstep: Six Stories of Dublin History* (Dublin, 2018), pp. 21–32.
13. Ruth McManus, 'How architect Herbert Simms transformed Dublin', RTÉ Brainstorm, 27 August 2021. Available at: https://www.rte.ie/brainstorm/2021/0826/1242953-herbert-simms-dublin-city-housing-architect-profile-ruth-mcmanus.
14. *Irish Independent*, 23 November 1932.
15. Redmond, *Show Us The Moon*, p. 29.
16. Alfred Barnard's *The Whisky Distilleries of the United Kingdom*, long sought after, was re-published by Aaron Barker Publishing as an e-book in 2013.
17. *Ibid.*
18. *The Harp*, May/June 1958. With thanks to the Guinness Archive.
19. Lynch and Vaizey, p. 92.
20. David Dickson, *Dublin: The Making of a Capital City* (London, 2014).
21. Dr. J. S. Corran, 'Brewing Malting and Distilling' in Elgy Gillespie (ed.), *The Liberties of Dublin* (Dublin, 1973), p. 88.
22. In the 1930s, with concern about the water quality and potential health implications for those taking part, the swim moved to Dollymount. Cyril J Smyth of the Dublin University Central Athletic Club is the foremost authority on the early history of the swim. See: *The Liffey Swim: The First Thirty Years 1920–1949* (Dublin, 2012).
23. Alfred Burgess, Bureau of Military History Witness Statement 1634, Military Archives.
24. Gordon Armstrong, *Samuel Beckett, W. B. Yeats, and Jack Yeats: Images and Words* (London, 1990), p. 164.

25. *The Irish Times*, 27 July 2019.
26. Terence de Vere White, *A Fretful Midge* (London, 1957), p. 153.
27. *Irish Independent*, 11 July 1928.
28. Margaret Ó hÓgartaigh, 'Internal tamponage, hockey parturition and mixed athletics' in *History Ireland*, (Vol. 15, No. 6).
29. *The Irish Times*, 22 October 2021.

3 FISHAMBLE STREET

1. *Sunday Press*, 24 September 1978.
2. From *The Newsletter of the Institute of Archaeologists of Ireland*.
3. Thomas F. Heffernan, *Wood Quay: The Clash Over Dublin's Viking Past* (Texas, 1988), p. 118.
4. My history of the 1988 anniversary is available to read in the *Dublin Inquirer*, 17 January 2018. An episode of the Three Castles Burning podcast also explores 1988.
5. *Maclean's*, 8 August 1988.
6. *The Annals of Ulster*, U902.
7. *Maclean's*, 8 August 1988.
8. *Irish Independent*, 22 September 1978.
9. *Evening Herald*, 1 December 1960.
10. *Irish Press*, 15 October 1955.
11. Patrick Abercrombie, *Dublin of the Future* (Dublin, 1922).
12. *Irish Independent*, 4 August 1972.
13. *Ibid*.
14. *Sunday Independent*, 6 August 1972.
15. As reported in *An Taisce: Ireland's Conservation Journal* (Vol. 1, No. 5). This document and other important historic documents have been uploaded to the Irish Left Archive on the Cedar Lounge Revolution website. See: https://cedarlounge.wordpress.com/2016/10/24/left-archive-occupation-news-1-12-june-1979-wood-quay-protest/.
16. Friends of Medieval Dublin, *Wood Quay: A European Heritage*. Posted to Irish Left Archive.
17. John Bradley (ed.), *Viking Dublin Exposed: The Wood Quay Saga* (Dublin, 1984), p. 41.
18. Heffernan, p. 56.
19. Ruth Johnson, *Viking Age Dublin* (Dublin, 2004), p. 30.
20. *Wood Quay Occupation News*, 12 June 1979. Posted to Irish Left Archive.
21. Bradley (ed.), p. 76.
22. *Ibid*., p. 58.
23. *Ibid*.

24. *The Irish Times*, 21 December 2015. Pat's work on Fishamble Street and Wood Quay is published in the lavishly illustrated *Viking Dublin: The Wood Quay Excavations* (Dublin, 2015).

25. The Heritage Council have published many significant excavation reports which were previously unpublished at https://www.heritage-council.ie/unpublished_excavations/section15.html. These include Fishamble Street reports from Patrick Wallace.

26. Horatio Townsend, *An Account of the Visit of Handel to Dublin* (Dublin, 1852), p. 2.

27. Jonathan Bardon, *Hallelujah: The Story of a Musical Genius and the City that brought his Masterpiece to Life* (Dublin, 2015), p. 5.

28. *Ibid*.

29. *Ibid*.

30. *Ibid*.

31. Howard E. Smither, *A History of the Oratorio Volume 2: The Oratorio in the Baroque Era* (North Carolina, 1977), p. 249.

32. Máire Kennedy, 'Disaster at the Music Hall, Fishamble Street, 6 February 1782', in *Dublin Historical Record* (Vol. 50, No. 2), p. 132.

33. *Dublin Inquirer*, 7 November 2018.

34. Heffernan, p. 104.

35. Frank McNally, *111 Places in Dublin That You Must Not Miss* (Köln, 2015).

36. Lawrence William White, 'Samuel Francis Stephenson', *Dictionary of Irish Biography* (Royal Irish Academy).

4   RATHMINES ROAD LOWER

1. Éamonn MacThomáis, *The Labour and the Royal* (Dublin, 1979).

2. See 'The Rathmines Accent' in *Dublin Review of Books*, October 2020, www.drb.ie.

3. C. S. Andrews, *Dublin Made Me* (Dublin, 2001), p. 3.

4. Lara Baker Whelan, *Class, Culture and Suburban Anxieties in the Victorian Era* (New York, 2010), p. 2.

5. Fionn Davenport's *Lonely Planet* guide to the city – occasionally updated – remains my go-to guide book to the city for visitors.

6. Kevin O'Shiel, Bureau of Military History Witness Statement 1770, Military Archives.

7. Séamas Ó Maitiú, *Dublin's Suburban Towns: 1834–1930* (Dublin, 2003), p. 33.

8. Susan Galavan, *Dublin's Bourgeois Homes: Building the Victorian Suburbs, 1850–1901* (London, 2017), p. 89.

9. Michael MacDonagh, *The Life of Daniel O'Connell* (Cassell, 1903), p. 292.

10. Ó Maitiú, p. 29.
11. *Ibid.*, p. 24.
12. Cathy Leeney and Deirdre McFeely, 'Social Class, Space and Containment in 1950s Ireland: Maura Laverty's Dublin Trilogy (1951–1952) in David Clare, Fiona McDonagh, Justine Nakase (eds.), *The Golden Thread: Irish Women Playwrights, Volume 1*, (Liverpool, 2021), p. 249.
13. Ó Maitiú, p. 50.
14. On the class composition of Rathmines see Mary Daly, *Dublin: The Deposed Capital: A Social and Economic History, 1860-1914* (Cork, 1984).
15. *Irish Independent*, 4 September 2020.
16. V. I. Lenin, 'Socialism and Religion', *Novaya Zhizn*, 3 December 1905.
17. *Freeman's Journal*, 7 December 1923.
18. Henry C. Murray, Bureau of Military History Witness Statement 601, Military Archives.
19. *Ibid.*
20. Michael Lynch, Bureau of Military History Witness Statement 511, Military Archives.
21. *Ibid.*
22. Las Fallon, 'Burning the Custom House', *thejournal.ie*, 25 May 2021. See also Las Fallon, *Dublin Fire Brigade and the Irish Revolution* (Dublin, 2013).
23. Alan John Ainsworth, 'Kodak House Dublin, Twentieth Century Society Building of the Month', August 2019. https://c20society.org.uk/building-of-the-month/kodak-house-dublin.
24. *Ibid.*
25. Eileen Costello, Bureau of Military History Witness Statement 1184, Military Archives.
26. Lucy McDiarmid, *The Irish Art of Controversy* (London, 2005), p. 63.
27. 'Anti-Enlistment Meeting Held at Beresford Place', Dublin Metropolitan Police, 13 December 1914, National Archives of Ireland.
28. Andrée Sheehy Skeffington, *Skeff: The Life of Owen Sheehy Skeffington, 1909–1970* (Dublin, 1991), p. 15.
29. *Mother Earth* was a publication edited by the Anarchist Emma Goldman. Colum's tribute to Francis Sheehy-Skeffington appeared in the June 1916 edition.
30. Joseph McKenna, *Guerrilla Warfare in the Irish War of Independence, 1919–1921* (North Carolina, 2011), p. 104.
31. David Nasaw, *Andrew Carnegie* (New York, 2006), p. 354.
32. Roger L. Kemp, *Cities and the Arts: A Handbook for Renewal* (North Carolina, 2004), p. 57.

33. *Irish Independent,* 20 March 1930.
34. *Ibid.*, 10 October 1929.
35. Ó Maitiú, p. 216.

5   SOUTH WILLIAM STREET

1. Pat Dargan, *Dublin Pubs* (Gloucestershire, 2018).
2. E. H. Mikhail (ed.), *The Art of Brendan Behan* (London, 1979), p. 19.
3. Robert Anthony Welch, *The Cold of May Day Monday: An Approach to Irish Literary History* (Oxford, 2014).
4. Robert O'Byrne, *The Irish Georgian Society: A Celebration* (Dublin, 2008), p. 190.
5. *Ibid.*
6. P. J. Raftery, 'Who Was Malton?' in *Dublin Historical Record* (Vol. 19, No. 4), p. 104.
7. *Ibid.*
8. Daniel Beaumont, 'James Malton' in *Dictionary of Irish Biography*, Royal Irish Academy.
9. Graham Hickey, 'Picking Through the Details of James Malton's Dublin' in Djinn von Noorden (ed.), *Malton's Views of Dublin: The Story of a Georgian City* (Dublin, 2021), p. 91.
10. C. T. McGready, *Dublin Street Names: Dated and Explained* (Dublin, 1892), p. 144.
11. C. P. Curran, 'Dublin Plaster Work' in *The Journal of the Royal Society of Antiquaries of Ireland* (Vol. 10, No. 1), p. 2.
12. Kathryn Milligan, 'A City of Rare Habits: James Malton's Dublin' in Djinn Von Noorden (ed.), *Malton's Views of Dublin: The Story of a Georgian City* (Dublin, 2021), p. 105.
13. Irish Georgian Society, 'City Assembly House - A History', https://www.igs.ie/conservation/project/city-assembly-house-a-history.
14. C. M. O'Keefe, *Life and Times of Daniel O'Connell Volume II* (Dublin, 1864), p. 666.
15. Kevin O'Shiel, Bureau of Military History Witness Statement 1770, Military Archives.
16. Marie Coleman, *The Irish Revolution: 1916–1923* (London, 2014), p. 60.
17. Comment by Dermot Bolger, Facebook, 15 December 2020.
18. In 2011, the brilliant Storymap initiative recorded Dubliners, native and new, telling stories about the city at interesting locations. One of the recorded stories is Leo talking about Bang Bang. Available to view at: https://www.youtube.com/watch?v=PeAH0D1KkoM.

19. Christine Casey, *Dublin: The City Within the Grand and Royal Canals and the Circular Road with the Phoenix Park* (London, 2005), p. 492.
20. *Ibid.*
21. *Evening Herald,* 11 June 1964.
22. Tommy Smith, 'Remembering Paddy' in *Martello* (Autumn 1997), pp. 24–26.
23. *Ibid.*
24. Ballagh, p. 154.
25. Críostóir Ó Floinn, *Van Gogh Chocolates: Poems and Translations* (Dublin, 2000), p. 19.
26. John Montague, *The Pear is Ripe: A Memoir* (Liberties, 2007).
27. *Sunday World*, 8 October 1978.
28. G. Ivan Morris, *In Dublin's Fair City* (London, 1947), p. 32.
29. *Ibid.*
30. Dara Gannon's 'Portrait of a Pub' appeared in the Irish special of *Stranger's Guide*, an award-winning travel publication. It can be read in full at: https://strangersguide.com/articles/portrait-of-a-pub-ireland/.
31. 'Eden Slots into the Hipster Triangle', *LovinDublin*, 20 December 2016.

6   PARNELL STREET EAST

1. *The Irish Times*, 28 January 2017.
2. Joseph Valente, *The Myth of Manliness in Irish National Culture, 1880–1922* (Illinois, 2011), P. 55.
3. *Ibid.*
4. Peter Sommrville-Large, *Dublin: The Fair City* (London, 1996), p. 219.
5. Richard J. Finneran, *W. B. Yeats: The Poems* (Volume 1) (New York, 1997), p. 537.
6. *Report of the O'Connell Monument Committee* (Dublin, 1888).
7. Sidney Kaplan, 'The Sculptural World of Augustus Saint-Gaudens', in *The Massachusetts Review* (Vol. 30, No. 1), p. 20.
8. *Ibid.*
9. *Ibid.*
10. *Ibid.*
11. Richard Kirkland, *Irish London: A Cultural History 1850–1916* (London, 2022), p. 63.
12. Helen Litton (ed.), *Kathleen Clarke: Revolutionary Woman* (Dublin, 2008), p. 6.
13. Dublin Metropolitan Police Movement of Extremist Files, 8 September 1915. National Archives of Ireland.

14. Sidney Czira, Bureau of Military History Witness Statement 909, Military Archives.
15. Dublin Civic Trust, *Parnell Street: A Vision for an Historic City Centre Street* (Dublin, 2011), p. 6.
16. Sebastian Barry, *The Pride of Parnell Street* (London, 2014).
17. Yee Chiang, *The Silent Traveller in London* (London, 2002), p. 1.
18. Donal Fallon, 'From Vietnam to Blanchardstown', *Come Here To Me!*, 7 May 2019. Available at: https://comeheretome.com/2019/05/07/from-vietnam-to-blanchardstown/.
19. *Ibid.*
20. Mark Maguire's 2004 thesis is available to read in full at MURAL: Maynooth University Research Archive Library. https://mural.maynoothuniversity.ie/view/ethesisauthor/Maguire=3AMark=3A=3A.html.
21. Siobhán Marie Kilfeather, *Dublin: A Cultural History* (Oxford, 2005), p. 219.
22. Joe Duffy, Freya McClements, *Children of the Troubles: The Untold Story of the Children Killed in the Troubles* (Dublin, 2019), p. 164.
23. Quoted in Brian Hanley, *The Impact of the Troubles on the Republic of Ireland, 1968–79: Boiling Volcano?* (Manchester, 2018).
24. Kevin C. Kearns, *Dublin Street Life & Lore: An Oral History* (Dublin, 1991).
25. Karl McDonald, 'Lady on the Rock: Tracing the phenomenon of Dublin's own *Venus de Milo*', *Totally Dublin,* 5 November 2012.
26. *The Irish Times,* 24 December 2013.
27. Eamonn Doyle overview at Michael Hoppen Gallery. Available at: https://www.michaelhoppengallery.com/artists/35-eamonn-doyle/overview/.

7 JAMES JOYCE STREET

1. From 'Report of the Paving Committee', Minutes of Dublin Corporation, 1921.
2. Finola Kennedy, *Frank Duff: A Life Story* (London, 2011), p. 80.
3. James Joyce, *Ulysses* (London, 1961 edition), p. 429.
4. Quoted in Desmond Clarke, *Dublin* (Batsford, 1977), p. 162.
5. Gogarty's influence over Joyce's work is explored by John Noel Turner and Marc A. Mamigonian in 'Solar Patriot: Oliver St. John Gogarty in *Ulysses*', *James Joyce Quarterly* (Vol. 41, No. 4) pp. 633–52.
6. Earnan P. Blythe, 'The Welsh Chapel in Dublin' in *Dublin Historical Record* (Vol. 14, No. 3), pp. 74–79.
7. Helena Molony, Bureau of Military History Witness Statement 391, Military Archives.

8. Gerry Smyth, *Music and Sound in the Life and Literature of James Joyce: James Noyce* (New York, 2020), p. 244.

9. Cyril Pearl, *Dublin in Bloomtime: the City James Joyce Knew* (Dublin, 1969), p. 10.

10. Joyce (1961), p. 429.

11. Leanne McCormick, *Regulating Sexuality: Women in twentieth-century Northern Ireland* (Manchester, 2013).

12. Joseph V. O'Brien, *Dear, Dirty Dublin: A City in Distress, 1899–1916* (California, 1982), p. 192.

13. For more on Grafton Street and prostitution historically see Donal Fallon 'Grafton Street 1870: "The street literally swarmed with women of loose character"' in *thejournal.ie*, 15 October 2017. Availableat: https://www. thejournal.ie/readme/grafton-street-1870-the-street-literally-swarmed-with-women-of-loose-character-3645126-Oct2017/.

14. Terry Fagan, *Monto: Madams, Murder and Black Coddle* (Dublin, 2000), p. 15.

15. O'Brien, p. 191.

16. Fagan, p. 32.

17. 2 Faithful Place, 1911 Census, National Archives of Ireland.

18. Augustine Ingoldsby, Bureau of Military History Witness Statement 582, Military Archives.

19. Breandán MacAodha, 'Was this a Social Revolution?' in Seán Ó Tuama (ed.), *The Gaelic League Idea* (Cork, 1972), p. 22.

20. Matthew Kelly, '....and WIllie Rooney spoke in Irish.' in *History Ireland* (Vol. 15, No. 1).

21. Jimmy Wren, *Crinan – Dublin: A History of 13 North Inner-City Streets* (Dublin, 1993).

22. 'The First Dáil Éireann, the North Dock and Phil Shanahan TD', East Wall For All, Available at http://www. eastwallforall.ie/?p=4298.

23. Luke Kelly, Bureau of Military History Witness Statement 165, Military Archives.

24. Thomas Pugh, Bureau of Military History Witness Statement 397, Military Archives.

25. Anne Dolan, 'Alfred (Alfie) Byrne' in the Dictionary of Irish Biography, Royal Irish Academy.

26. Thomas Leahy, Bureau of Military History Witness Statement 660 Military Archives.

27. Dan Breen, Bureau of Military History Witness Statement 1739, Military Archives.

28. Phil Shanahan Intelligence File, Castle File No.1791.

29. Ronan Sheehan, Brendan Walsh, *Dublin: The Heart of the City* (Dublin, 2016), p. 42.

30. 1905 Report of the Paving Committee, Dublin Corporation Minute Books. Dublin City Library and Archives.

31. *Dublin Inquirer*, 26 January 2022.

32. These tensions are well explored in Maurice Curtis, *A Challenge to Democracy: Militant Catholicism in Modern Ireland* (Dublin, 2010).

33. Frank Duff, *Baptism of Fire* (Dublin, 1961), p. 15.

34. Sheehan and Walsh, p. 46.

35. Luddy, *Prostitution and Irish Society*, p. 216.

36. Sheehan and Walsh, p. 46.

37. Seán O'Casey, *The Story of the Irish Citizen Army* (Dublin, 1919), p. 55.

38. *Ibid.*, *The Plough and the Stars*, 1926.

39. *Ibid.*, *Inishfallen, Fare Thee Well* (New York, 1956), p. 240.

40. A fascinating *An Irishman's Diary* on Hoddy can be found in *The Irish Times,* 7 May 2011. Hoddy was the regular jazz writer, and occasional theatre reviewer, for the same paper.

41. Brian Singleton, *ANU Productions: The Monto Cycle* (Cambridge, 2016).

42. Rosanna Negrotti, *Joyce's Dublin: An Illustrated Commentary* (London, 2000), p. 109.

43. Mary Corbally, *Diamond Memories* (Dublin, 1980), p. 36.

8   SHIP STREET

1. Patrick Carroll, *Science, Culture, and Modern State Formation* (California, 2006), p. 112.

2. Maria Johnston, 'Walking Dublin: Contemporary Irish Poets in the City' in Fran Brearton, Alan Gillis (eds.), *The Oxford Handbook of Modern Irish Poetry* (Oxford, 2012), p. 501.

3. Food historian Máirtín Mac Con Iomaire has explored some of these street names, both urban and suburban. See 'Dublin's Street Names Offer Clues to the City's Culinary History', *Dublin Inquirer*, 15 August 2018.

4. Mr. Jonathan Pim, 'Report on Dairy Yards' in *The Dublin Journal of Medical Science* (Vol.VCVI, 1893), p. 328.

5. Eamon Broy, Bureau of Military History Witness Statement 1280, Military Archives.

6. Andrews, p. 5.

7. Somerville-Large, p. 236.

8. Mitchell, p. 10.

9. Maurice Craig, *Dublin 1660–1860* (Dublin, 1969), p. 280.

10. Seamus Daly, Bureau of Military History Witness Statement 360, Military Archives.

11. *The Irish Citizen*, 22 June 1912.

12. *Ibid.*

13. Hanna Sheehy-Skeffington, 'Reminiscences of an Irish Suffragette', quoted in Siobhán Marie Kilfeather, *Dublin: A Cultural History* (Oxford, 2005), p. 175.

14. Leah Levenson, Jerry H. Natterstad, *Hanna Sheehy-Skeffington: Irish Feminist* (New York, 1986), p. 37.

15. Michael D. Higgins, Speech at the unveiling of a plaque dedicated to Irish Suffragettes, Dublin Castle, 13 June 2018.

16. The events of Black Friday are well explored in Sophia A. van Wingerden, *The Women's Suffrage Movement in Britain, 1866-1928* (New York, 1999).

17. Margaret Gowen (ed.), *Conservation Plan: Dublin City Walls and Defences* (Dublin, 2004), p. 25.

18. Patrick Wallace, 'The Archaeology of Ireland's Viking-Age Towns' in Dáibhí Ó Cróinín, *A New History of Ireland, Volume I: Prehistoric and Early Ireland* (Oxford, 2005), pp. 814–40.

19. Christine Casey, *Dublin: The City Within the Grand and Royal Canals and the Circular Road with the Phoenix Park* (Yale, 2005), p. 19.

20. Jonathan Bardon, *Hallelujah – The story of a musical genius and the city that brought his masterpiece to life* (Dublin, 2016).

21. Walter Scott, *The Works of Jonathan Swift: Dean of St. Patrick's Cathedral* (Boston, 1884), p.123.

22. Peter Costello, *Dublin Castle in the Life of the Irish Nation* (Dublin, 1999), p. 15.

23. *The Irish Builder*, 17 February 1866.

24. Cormac Ó Gráda, 'Irish immigration then and now' in Francesca Fauri (ed.), *The History of Migration in Europe: Perspectives from Economics, Politics and Sociology* (New York, 2015), 154-172.

25. *Evening Herald,* 8 April 1976.

26. *Ibid.*

27. Vincent Caprani's *Rowdy Rhymes and Rec-im-itations: Doggerel for a Departed Dublin* (Dublin, 1982) is an essential read for all interested in Dublin's oral tradition. Irish Life and Lore carried out an oral history with Vincent that included some observations on Italian Dublin. See https://www.irishlifeandlore.com/.

28. *The Irish Times,* 3 November 2009.

29. *Ibid.*

30. Helena Molony, Bureau of Military History Witness Statement 391, Military Archives.
31. Edward Handley, Bureau of Military History Witness Statement 625, Military Archives.
32. *The Irish Bulletin,* 27 September 1919.
33. *The Irishman,* 16 August 1919.
34. P. H. Fox, 'The Causes of Enteric Fever in the Dublin Garrison', *The Dublin Journal of Medical Science* (Vol. XC, July to December, 1890), p. 503.
35. *Ibid.*
36. *Irish Independent,* 5 February 2022.
37. Chris Reid has done some very interesting work in the broader area around oral history recollections and social history. See http://www.chrisreidartist.com/.

9   CHURCH STREET

1. Dickson, p. 13.
2. George Aloysius Little, *Dublin Before the Vikings: An Adventure in Discovery* (Dublin, 1957), p. 144.
3. Michael O'Sullivan, *Brendan Behan: A Life* (Dublin, 1999), p. 12.
4. Cormac Ó Gráda, *Ireland Before and After the Famine: Explorations in Economic History, 1800–1925* (Manchester, 1993), p. 43.
5. J. D. Herbert, *Irish Varieties, for the Last Fifty Years: Written from Recollections* (Dublin, 1836), p. 83.
6. William Curry, *The Picture of Dublin, or Stranger's Guide to the Irish Metropolis* (London, 1835), p. 184.
7. *Ibid.,* p. 160.
8. *British Medical Journal,* 28 September 1861.
9. *The Irish Times,* 26 August 1919.
10. *Freeman's Journal,* 29 April 1878.
11. *The Irish Times,* 29 April 1878.
12. *Freeman's Journal,* 29 April 1878.
13. *Ibid.*
14. Tom Geraghty, Trevor Whitehead, *Dublin Fire Brigade: A history of the brigade, the fires and the emergencies* (Dublin, 2004), p. 62.
15. *Ibid.,* p. 64.
16. Pakenham and Pakenham, p. 4.
17. W. H. Bartlett, *Picturesque Ireland: Historical and Descriptive* (New York, 1890), p. 15.
18. *Ibid.*

19. Thomas J. Cummins, *Remarkable Trials of all Countries* (New York, 1867), p. 48.
20. R. R. Madden, *The Life and Times of Robert Emmet, Esq* (Dublin, 1847), p. 286.
21. Peadar O'Donnell, *Not Yet Emmet: A Wreath on the Grave of Sean Murray* (Dublin, 1985).
22. Sheila Carden, *The Alderman: Alderman Tom Kelly (1868–1942) and Dublin Corporation* (Dublin, 207), p. 114.
23. *Ibid.*
24. O'Brien, p. 149.
25. Chris Corlett, 'The Church Street Disaster, September 1913', *History Ireland* (Vol. 17, No. 2), p. 30.
26. Jim Larkin, *Larkin's Scathing Indictment of Dublin Sweaters* (Dublin, 1914), p. 4.
27. James Plunkett, 'Jim Larkin' in J. W. Boyle (ed.), *Leaders and Workers* (Dublin, 1965), p. 85.
28. O'Brien, p. 98.
29. Sean Farrell Moran, *Patrick Pearse and the Politics of Redemption: The Mind of the Easter Rising* (Washington, 1998), p. 67.
30. Carden, p. 113.
31. *Ibid.*
32. *thejournal.ie*, 31 December 2013.
33. Mark Lawrence Schrad, *Smashing the Liquor Machine: A Global History of Prohibition* (Oxford, 2021), p. 309.
34. A new public housing scheme on nearby North King Street will be named in Seán Foster's honour. The deaths of Seán and other child victims of the Rising is examined in Joe Duffy's *Children of the Rising: The Untold Story of the Young Lives Lost during Easter 1916* (Dublin, 2015).
35. Eamonn Morkan, Bureau of Military History Witness Statement 411, Military Archives.
36. Wally Cassidy's photo collection is published by Cafe Royal Books, 2017. Bill Barich's observation comes from Bill Barich, *A Pint of Plain: Tradition, Change, and the Fate of the Irish Pub* (New York, 2009)
37. Interview with Subset, *Green News*. Available at: https://greennews.ie/subset-climate-art-dublin/.

10 EUSTACE STREET

1. *The Irish Times*, 16 April 2014.
2. Robin Usher, *Protestant Dublin, 1660–1760: Architecture and Iconography* (London, 2012), p. 171.

3. Colm Lennon, 'The Changing Face of Dublin, 1550-1750' in Peter Clark, Raymond Gillespie (eds.), *Two Capitals: London and Dublin: 1500–1840* (Oxford, 2001), p. 50.

4. Quoted in Frank McDonald, *A Little History of the Future of Dublin* (Dublin, 2021), p. 119.

5. Paul Knox, *Palimpsests: Biographies of 50 City Districts* (Basel, 2012), p. 236.

6. *Irish Independent*, 13 November 1998.

7. Rupert James Rowton, *The Light of the West* (London, 1869), p. 394.

8. Jim Smyth, *The Men of No Property: Irish Radicals and Popular Politics in the Late Eighteenth Century* (London, 1998), p. 135.

9. William Theobald Wolfe Tone (ed.), *Memoirs of Theobald Wolfe Tone: Volume One* (London, 1837), p. 50.

10. Marianne Elliot, *Wolfe Tone* (Liverpool, 2012), p. 133.

11. Richard Robert Madden, *The United Irishmen, Their Lives and Times, Volume 1* (Dublin, 1858), p. 228.

12. Peter Collins, *Who Fears to Speak of 98? Commemoration and the Continuing impact of the United Irishmen* (Belfast, 2004), p. 133.

13. Martyn J. Powell, 'Political Toasting in Eighteenth-Century Ireland' in *History: The Journal of the Historical Association* (Vol. 91, Issue 304), pp. 508–29.

14. *Ibid.*

15. Donal Fallon, 'Olaudah Equiano's Irish Friends', *Dublin Inquirer*, 15 August 2018.

16. David Booey, *Autobiographical Writings by Early Quaker Women* (Cambridge, 2004), p. 5.

17. Richard S. Harrison, 'Irish Quaker Perspectives on the Anti-Slavery Movement' in *The Journal of the Friends Historical Society* (Vol. 56, No. 2), p. 114.

18. Letter from William Lloyd Garrison to George W. Benson, Boston, 22 March 1842 in Walter M. Merrill (ed.), *The Letters of William Lloyd Garrison: Volume III* (Massachusetts, 1973), p. 61.

19. Frederick Douglass, *Narrative of the Life of Frederick Douglass* (Boston, 1845), p. 1.

20. *Freeman's Journal*, 13 September 1845.

21. *Ibid.*

22. Quoted in Christine Kinealy (ed.), *Frederick Douglass and Ireland: In His Own Words* (New York, 2018).

23. Patricia J. Ferreira, 'Frederick Douglass in Ireland: The Dublin Edition of His "Narrative"' in *New Hibernia Review/Iris Éireannach Nua* (Vol. 5, No. 1), p. 63.

24. *Ibid.*
25. David Kavanagh, 'IFI20: Finding home in Temple Bar', IFI Blog, http://irishfilminstitute.blogspot.com/.
26. Ruth Barton, *Irish National Cinema* (London, 2004), p. 36.
27. Marie Colman entry on James Montgomery, Dictionary of Irish Biography, Royal Irish Academy.
28. *Sunday Press*, 28 November 1972.
29. *Irish Examiner*, 3 June 1967.
30. John Cooney, *John Charles McQuaid: Ruler of Catholic Ireland* (Dublin, 1999), p. 279.
31. *Ibid.*
32. *Report of the engineers to whom were referred plans placed before the council for the purification of the Liffey and the abatement of the nuisance arising therefrom* (Dublin, 1874), p. 13.
33. *Irish Independent*, 29 November 1996.
34. Hannah Moskowitz, *Sick Kids in Love* (New York, 2019).
35. Gillian Tait, *111 Places in Edinburgh that You Shouldn't Miss* (Köln, 2016), p. 41.
36. Anne Simpson, *Blooming Dublin: Choice, Change and Contradictions* (Dublin, 1991), p. 16.
37. John Stephenson, formerly of the Project Arts Centre, penned an excellent plea for unity from cultural institutions in *The Irish Times*, 6 July 2021.

11 PEARSE STREET (TO WESTLAND ROW)

1. Depending on the document or occasion, it was Patrick Henry (P. H.) Pearse or Pádraig Mac Piarais, but never the halfway house of Pádraig Pearse.
2. Desmond Ryan, Bureau of Military History Witness Statement 724, Military Archives.
3. Séamus Conboy, Changing Dublin Street Names, 1880's to 1940's, in *Dublin Historical Record* (Vol. 64, No. 2), p. 205.
4. Stephen Moore, *A History of Pearse Street Station* (Dublin, 2016), p. 17.
5. Barry Kennerk, *The Peeler's Notebook: Policing Victorian Dublin – Mad Dogs, Duels and Dynamite* (Cork, 2019), p. 18.
6. Anastasia Dukova, *A History of the Dublin Metropolitan Police and its Colonial Legacy* (London, 2016), p. 139.
7. *The Irish Times*, 24 March 1904.
8. Moore, p. 32.
9. *Irish Independent*, 8 May 1905.

10. The Burgh Quay Sad Calamity was written by Robert Costello. With thanks to the late Tony Behan.

11. Jim Phelan, *The Name's Phelan* (London, 1934), p. 151.

12. *Ibid.*

13. *Ibid.*

14. Dublin Metropolitan Police, 'Movement of Extremist Files', CDO/JD/2/243, National Archives of Ireland.

15. Eamon Broy, Bureau of Military History Witness Statement 1280, Military Archives.

16. James J. Slattery, Bureau of Military History Witness Statement 445, Military Archives.

17. See profile of Joseph Connolly by Donal Fallon in *Saothar* (No. 41, 2016), the journal of the Irish Labour History Society.

18. Las Fallon, 'Man of fire: Captain Thomas Purcell' in *Firecall,* 2017.

19. Tom Geraghty, Trevor Whitehead, *The Dublin Fire Brigade* (Dublin, 2004), p. 2.

20. A. P. Behan, 'A Triple Tragedy in Dublin, the Pearse Street Fire, 1936', *Dublin Historical Record* (Vol. 50, No. 1), p. 10.

21. *Sunday Independent*, 25 January 1975.

22. *Dublin and its Environs* (Dublin, 1846), p. 138.

23. Hugh Hunt, *The Abbey: Ireland's National Theatre, 1904-1978* (Dublin, 1979), p. 4.

24. Frank McDonald, *The Destruction of Dublin* (Dublin 1985), p. 45.

25. Róisín Ní Ghairbhí, *Willie Pearse: 16 Lives* (Dublin, 2015).

26. 27 Pearse Street, Dublin Civic Trust. http://www.dublincivictrust.ie/building-projects/pearse-st.

27. Sean Farrell Moran, *Patrick Pearse and the Politics of Redemption: The Mind of the Easter Rising* (Washington, 1997), p. 47.

28. In 2016, Charles Moore of Britain's *Daily Telegraph* would go as far as to compare P. H. Pearse to the so-called Islamic State. 'Islamic State and the Easter Rising', 28 April 2016.

29. Don Gifford and Robert J. Seidman (eds.), *Ulysses Annotated: Revised and Expanded Edition* (New York, 1974), p. 108.

30. Patrick J. Stephenson, 'The Antient Concert Rooms', *Dublin Historical Record* (Vol. 5, No. 1), pp. 1–14.

31. *Ibid.*

32. E. H. Mikhail (ed.), *Lady Gregory: Interviews and Recollections* (London, 1977), p. 62.

33. Gregory A. Schirmer, *Reviews and Essays of Austin Clarke* (Buckinghamshire, 1995), p. 23.

34. *Ibid.*

12 MOORE STREET

1.   *Irish Independent,* 15 October 1966.
2.   McDonald, p. 78.
3.   *Irish Independent*, 15 December 1967.
4.   Mitchell, p. 1.
5.   *Ibid.*, p. 64.
6.   Kearns (1991), p. 11.
7.   *Ibid.*, p. 118.
8.   Séamus Scully, *The Dublin Rover* (Dublin, 1991), p. 13.
9.   *Ibid.*, p. 17.
10. Kennerk (2012), p. 21.
11. *Evening Herald*, 30 October 1981.
12. *The Irish Builder and Engineer*, 15 March 1861.
13. Erika Hanna, *Modern Dublin: Urban Change and the Irish Past, 1957–1973* (Oxford, 2013), p. 36.
14. *Ibid.*
15. *Irish Independent*, 24 October 1958.
16. *Evening Herald*, 16 July 1959.
17. While Molly Malone may be fictional, an eagle eye will notice Mrs. Brown lives on 'James Larkin Court', a street named after a very real working class icon. O'Carroll says much on Moore Street in Brian Beacom, *The Real Mrs. Brown: The Authorised Biography of Brendan O'Carroll* (London, 2013).
18. *Evening Herald*, 4 September 1985.
19. Kennerk (2012), p. 29.
20. Joe Lee's film includes the final interview with Tony Gregory TD. It can be viewed in full at www.joelee.ie.
21. *Sunday Press*, 26 January 1986.
22. *Irish Independent,* 3 January 2009.
23. Róisín Curé, *Dublin in Sketches and Stories* (Dublin, 2021).
24. Isabelle Torrance and Donncha O'Rourke, 'Classics and Irish Politics: Introduction' in *Classics and Irish Politics, 1916–2016* (Oxford, 2020), p. 5.
25. Desmond Ryan, Bureau of Military History Witness Statement 724, Military Archives.
26. Paul Rouse, *Sport and Ireland: A History* (Oxford, 2015), p. 36.
27. Donal Fallon, 'Ghosts of the Paris Commune', *Jacobin*, 4 April 2016. Available at: https://jacobinmag.com/2016/04/james-con-nolly-paris-commune-easter-rising-tactics.
28. Kennerk (2012), p. 61.
29. Scully, p. 90.
30. *Ibid.*, p. 92.s

Index